Modern Wrestling

MODERN WRESTLING

A Primer for Wrestlers,
Parents, and Fans

Benjamin W. Niebel
and
Douglas A. Niebel

The Pennsylvania State University Press
University Park and London

Library of Congress Cataloging in Publication Data

Niebel, Benjamin W.
Modern wrestling.

Includes bibliography and index.
1. Wrestling.   I.   Niebel, Douglas A.,
1947–   .   II.   Title.
GV1195.N53   796.8'12   82-7478
ISBN 0-271-00323-5 cloth
ISBN 0-271-00328-6 paper
AACR2

Contents

Contents

Preface

This book is dedicated to the millions of parents, relatives, and friends who have agonized while a member of their family or a close friend was in competition with an adversary who appeared to be immeasurably bigger and stronger. This volume focuses on both scholastic and collegiate wrestling, and has been written for wrestlers, parents, and other participants and spectators. It should help you appreciate one of America's most rapidly growing sports. Certainly, after reading this book you will have a much better understanding of how the wrestler should train, control his weight, and prepare himself both mentally and physically for each contest. You will understand the principal holds and how they can result in mechanical advantage over an opponent. It is anticipated that by reading and studying this volume you will also develop a deep respect for the young men who participate in wrestling—one of the most demanding sports.

The authors wish to acknowledge the people who read this manuscript and provided many constructive criticisms. Notable among these are Dr. William H. Koll, a member of the Wrestling Hall of Fame and past wrestling coach at The Pennsylvania State University; Thad Turner, present wrestling coach at Lehigh University, who was named by the National Wrestling Coaches Association as the 1979 College Coach of the Year; Rich Lorenzo, present wrestling coach at Penn State; John Fritz, past NCAA champion and present assistant wrestling coach at Penn State; David H. Clelland, past wrestling coach at Greenville High School and member of the Pennsylvania Coaches Hall of Fame; Dr. Edgar H. Knapp, past scholastic wrestling coach; Charles Kimzey, certified collegiate and scholastic wrestling official; Dr. Elsworth Buskirk, director of Penn State's Human Performance Laboratory; Dr. Chauncey Morehouse, professor of physical education at Penn State; Dr. Daniel Gould, assistant professor of health, physical education and recreation at Michigan State; and Drs. John B. Dalbor, Samuel S. Lestz, and Robert Noll, wrestling buffs.

The authors acknowledge with thanks Brett Tyson and Dwight E. Rotz, who prepared artwork and photography in connection with illustrating the principal holds, and William Wright, Douglas Barger, Joe Lenker, and David McCollum (wrestling coach at Bermudian Springs) for demonstrating the holds. Appreciation is extended to Judy Berg and Eleanor Tyson for typing the manuscript.

1

Introduction

Far better it is to dare mighty things, to win glorious triumphs, even though checkered by failure, than to take rank with those poor spirits who neither enjoy much nor suffer much, because they live in the gray twilight that knows not victory nor defeat.

—Theodore Roosevelt

As an organized sport, amateur wrestling contributes in a positive way to the total development of the athlete. This sport develops all his muscles and promotes quickness, agility, and endurance. It also develops mental discipline, builds self-confidence, and prepares the participant to accept both success and failure. It is open to all who wish to participate regardless of height, weight, or physical attributes. On occasion, there have been successful high-school and college wrestlers who were blind, without the use of an arm, or without the use of a foot. Unlike many other sports, the size of the squad reporting for practice is no deterrent. It is always disturbing to a young high-school hopeful to be "cut" because the nature of a sport does not permit a large squad. This need not happen in wrestling—in this sport, the more the merrier.

In wrestling there is little similarity between amateur and professional competition. Amateur wrestling involves contests where skilled, conditioned athletes participate in competitive sport of the highest order. Professional wrestling, on the other hand, has degenerated into a sham affair for the sole purpose of entertainment, and showmanship often replaces skill in matches. The wrestlers often wear unusual costumes and take on descriptive names. The match (it is never a contest) frequently pairs a "villain," who appears to kick, bite, and gouge his opponent, against a "hero," who is usually the declared winner. It is important for the reader to understand that this book is written with reference to "amateur" scholastic and collegiate wrestling.

CRITERIA FOR SUCCESS

The successful wrestler must attain and simultaneously utilize four fundamental qualities: skill, strength, condition, and desire. These four requirements are not independent of each other. They must be tied together cohesively so that, when in competition, the athlete employs to his full capability all four of these qualities. For example, a wrestler with much skill but little strength would not be continually successful, even though he had great desire and was in superb condition.

Proficient wrestling requires a large number of specialized skills. The many maneuvers of takedowns, escapes, reversals, and pinning combinations, to be executed as a smooth rhythmic sequence, can only be accomplished by a skilled athlete. However, like most athletic skills, these skills can be acquired by any reasonably coordinated young man who is willing to spend the practice time necessary for the realization of smooth performance. Diligent practice is the key.

Strength is as fundamental to the wrestler as speed is to the 100-meter sprinter. However, strength is similar to skill in that it can be developed. Perhaps the most efficient way to do this is through a program of weight lifting. The weight-lifting exercises the wrestler might employ include bench presses, rowing exercises, push-ups, presses behind the neck, chin-ups, hang-cleans, leg lifting, and leg thrusts. In Chapter 6 we will discuss the kind of training necessary for the development of both strength and stamina.

The third fundamental requirement for the successful wrestler is condition or stamina. As with skill and strength, this can be gained through dedication. However, it should be noted that conditioning is of greater importance in wrestling than it is in many other contact sports. There is very little time to rest or relax during a wrestling match. To be successful, the wrestler must be prepared to exert himself at an all-out, 100-percent pace for most of the seven minutes of the match (six minutes in scholastic wrestling). The best way to develop stamina and condition is to improve the cardiorespiratory function, and this can best be accomplished by regular running, followed by routine conditioning exercises. The conditioned wrestler should be able to run a brisk mile without feeling winded or tired.

The last of the four basic requirements for success in wrestling is desire. Desire implies the development of feelings which cause one to strive for victory regardless of the obstacles. It can be thought of as being synonymous with mental toughness and courage, and these characteristics can only be obtained through mental discipline. We will discuss in detail the necessary psychological preparation for success in Chapter 7.

SUMMARY

The individual considering participation in this sport should understand that the four qualifications necessary for success as a wrestler—skill, strength, condition, and desire—can readily be developed. He should realize this sport will do much to strengthen his body and provide self-confidence. In addition, it should be encouraging to know that no other body-contact sport has such a low serious injury rate. The vast proportion of injuries received by wrestlers are sprains, pulls, bruises, minor contusions, and mat burns.[1]

If you are a wrestler, you should be congratulated on selecting a demanding sport that will bring out the best in you. If you are a parent, you should appre-

[1]Robert G. Bubb, "Survey of Injuries to Interscholastic Wrestlers in Selected Pennsylvania High Schools, 1966–1967 Season" (M.Ed. thesis, The Pennsylvania State University, 1967).

ciate the fact that your son is participating in a sport that will develop his body, mind, and spirit. If you are a coach or a referee, you should be congratulated for utilizing your skills, philosophies, and talents to teach young men the importance of self-discipline, the rewards of physical and mental conditioning, and the thrill of demanding competition.

2

A Brief History

And Jacob was left alone; and a man wrestled with him until daybreak.
—Genesis 32:24

No other organized sport has a lengthier history than does wrestling. Carvings and drawings estimated to be between 15,000 and 20,000 years old, found in caves in France, illustrate wrestlers in hold and leverage positions. Much factual information about wrestling has been obtained from Egypt because of the excellent condition of the paintings, writings, and carvings found in the elaborate tombs Egyptians prepared for their kings and officials. We know that wrestling had already reached a high stage of development in Egypt about five thousand years ago, since paintings of wrestlers that date to approximately 2500 B.C. have been discovered in the tombs of the Fifth Dynasty. In the tomb of a vizier named Ptah-hotep, six different wrestling holds are shown, and it has been estimated that in the temple-tombs at Beni Hasan as many as 466 different holds are illustrated.[1]

Wrestling has also been popular in the Orient, particularly in Japan, from very early times. The first *recorded* wrestling match in Japan took place in 23 B.C. The national style of wrestling in Japan is sumo, where the object is either to throw the opponent to the ground or to force him out of the boundary lines of the mat. Originally, sumo permitted the use of almost any type of blow to force an opponent off the mat, including kicking and punching. Eventually, a formal ritual and rules were established. Since there are no weight classes, size as well as strength are distinct assets. Sumo has for years been a popular spectator sport in Japan. Audiences as large as the arena can accommodate (in some cases, 100,000 or more) will attend a well-publicized professional wrestling match.

An outgrowth of wrestling is the Japanese method of self-defense known as "ju-jitsu," which had its origin in the twelfth century and since has developed as a separate art. Judo, which also originated in Japan, is a modern form of ju-jitsu. Fundamentally, judo is a personal-defense methodology that uses a combination

[1]Don Sayenga, "The Oldest Sport," *Amateur Wrestling News,* September 28, 1978.

of throws and controlling holds. At the XVIII Olympiad in Tokoyo in 1964, judo was included in the program to honor the host country.

Wrestling matches were described by the Greek poet Homer and formed one of the features of the pentathlon, or fivefold contest, at the Greek public games. The Greek poet Pindar describes how the Gods Zeus and Cronus wrestled for possession of the universe along the river Alpheus at Olympia. Zeus was victorious and the first Olympic festival was held in 776 B.C. in commemoration of his victory. It was in the 18th Olympiad in 704 B.C. that wrestling was introduced into the Olympic Games as a major sport. Most of us today think of track and field events as the contests that are emphasized at the Olympic Games. We should be aware that wrestling was a principal event in the early version of these athletic contests, as well.

One of the most famous Greek wrestlers was the philosopher Plato, who won many prizes for wrestling as a young man. He participated as a wrestler in the Isthmian Games, one of four major Panhellenic festivals. His real name was Aristoelas, but, because he was a wrestler as well as a philosopher, he was given the name "Plato," meaning "Broad Shoulders."

After the conquest of the Greek Empire by the Romans, the sport degenerated into violent gladiatorial contests where the loser often did not survive. Instead of using only strength and skill, each gladiator was armed with a weapon capable of inflicting death or permanent bodily harm. However, the gladiators of this era did rely upon the courage, stamina, physical strength, and skills of wrestling.

The impact of the Olympic Games spread throughout Europe with the growth of the Roman Empire. Of course, the gladiatorial contests held in Rome had an influence on the style, regulations, and manner of matches conducted on the continent. It was in this era that the catch-as-catch-can style of wrestling was born—the wrestler may "catch" any hold he "can." Thus, the style was completely free—no holds barred. The contestant was free to grasp and hold any part of the anatomy of his opponent or what he was wearing—belt, toga, loincloth, shirt, or whatever.

In the Napoleonic period the French developed a style which, today, is identified as "Greco-Roman." This style requires a catch and hold; however, no holds on the legs are permitted, nor is tripping allowed. Throws are attempted from the standing position only, in an effort to score a fall. This occurs when one of the contestants throws his opponent to the mat so that the points of both shoulders touch the mat together. Greco-Roman wrestling is still used extensively in Europe and is sponsored in the Olympic Games, as is catch-as-catch-can or free-style. It is used in the United States, but to a much lesser degree than is free-style.

In both North and South America, Indians included wrestling in their sport activities long before Christopher Columbus set foot in the New World. Wrestling continued to be popular in Europe and throughout the world, and even the most prestigious people participated in the sport. A contest held in 1520 between Henry VIII of England and Francis I of France—the so-called "Cloth of Gold" meeting—has been reported in sporting annals, but existing records do not clearly describe the outcome. George Washington and Abraham Lincoln were both acknowledged as skilled wrestlers.

Today, wrestling remains a popular international sport, and is the national sport of several countries including Iran, Mongolia, Turkey, Iceland, and Switzerland.

MODERN WRESTLING

By the beginning of the twentieth century the "catch-as-catch-can" style of wrestling, which is more commonly referred to as "free-style," had become so popular in the United States that an amateur national championship was held annually and collegiate wrestling programs were organized as well. The free-style contest, unlike Greco-Roman, permitted tripping and single- and double-leg tackling. Wrestlers were also permitted to take holds below the waist and to use the legs as scissors.[2]

In 1900 the first intercollegiate match—between Yale and the University of Pennsylvania—was held. Soon, other eastern schools began collegiate wrestling, and in 1904 a group of eastern colleges and universities formed the Eastern Intercollegiate Wrestling Conference. This group established the first set of rules and regulations to be used in competition, and in 1905 they held their first tournament.

A major problem in those early days of collegiate wrestling was how to decide a winner when neither contestant had been able to score a fall. The procedure was to add a second period, usually three minutes in duration. The first period was always considerably longer. (For example, Amateur Athletic Union [AAU] bouts were somewhere between nine and thirty minutes in length.) If no fall occurred at the end of the second period, two judges (one from each team) plus the referee voted to determine the winner. A decision was based on both "aggressiveness" and "form and work." As might be expected, these criteria were difficult to evaluate objectively and many bouts ended in a tie or draw.

A result of the regular meetings of the Eastern Intercollegiate Wrestling Conference was a new plan for determining the winner. When there was no fall, the decision was awarded to the contestant who had the greatest amount of "time advantage." Thus, the wrestler who was "in control" longer was deemed the winner.

In 1919 the collegiate rules were modified so that contestants wrestled three periods of three minutes each in duration. They started the first period in a neutral position; one contestant started the second period from a control position; and in the last period, the other contestant took a control position.

In 1927 a Wrestling Rules Committee was established by the National Collegiate Athletic Association (NCAA). This committee, chaired by Dr. R. G. Clapp—at the time, chairman of the Physical Education Department at the University of Nebraska—was instrumental in the sport's development at both the collegiate and scholastic levels. Perhaps the most significant accomplishment of this group was the development of a "point" system for scoring a match when no fall occurs. This change made contests much more exciting, particularly from a spectator's point of view.

From eastern schools, wrestling spread rapidly to the midwestern and southwestern colleges and universities. In the early 1930s, the sport became ex-

---

[2]Current rules in free-style wrestling do not permit wrestlers to scissor the legs around the head or body.

7

tremely popular in Oklahoma. In the 1936 national collegiate tournament, the top three finishers were all from Oklahoma schools: Oklahoma State, first; Central State, runner-up; and the University of Oklahoma, third.

After World War II, the sport became increasingly popular across the United States, both at the collegiate and scholastic levels. In some geographic areas wrestling consistently drew larger crowds than basketball. This was especially true in sections of Oklahoma, Iowa, Pennsylvania, New York, Ohio, and New Jersey.

Today, no school or geographic area has a monopoly on the number of tournament champions. For example, in Pennsylvania in the period between 1950 and 1960, the majority of the state high-school champions came from "District Six" or "District Seven," both considered to be real "hot beds" of wrestling. Year after year, the majority of the state finalists came from these two areas; but today the state champions and runner-ups are distributed throughout the state of Pennsylvania. With the wide distribution of talent, improvement in the established rules, superior coaching and better equipment and facilities, the sport continues to grow.

3

Rules and Regulations

The strongest is never strong enough to be always the master, unless he transforms strength into right and obedience into duty.
—Jean Jacques Rousseau (1712–1778)

As we learned in the previous chapter, a Wrestling Rules Committee was established by the National Collegiate Athletic Association (NCAA) in 1927. There was a real need for agreement on such matters as participants' weights, length of bouts, fouls, determination of a winner, size of mat, and so forth, since there was no uniformity across the country on any of these parameters. Today, the sport is highly organized. There is an NCAA Wrestling Committee with three divisions: university, college, and junior college. A National Wrestling Coaches Association and a National Wrestling Committee Association have also been established. The committees oversee awards (including All-American), rules advisory, the East-West match, public relations, finance, membership, publication of the Handbook, and selection of the United States Wrestling Federation representative.

At the interscholastic level, the National Federation of State High School Associations prepares a high-school wrestling rule book. Individual state associations have the option of whether or not to adopt these rules. Pennsylvania and Virginia are examples of states that do use the National Federation's rules in their interscholastic wrestling programs.

Although it is not the purpose of this chapter to discuss every high-school and college rule and regulation, we do want to cover those that will help you to better understand and enjoy the bouts that you witness. Primarily, the rules and regulations for the two levels of competition are very much alike. A general discussion of the two sets of rules follows.

In high-school wrestling, there are usually twelve weight classes, whereas there are ten collegiate weight classes. At the time of the weigh-in before the match, the wrestler may weigh no more than the weight in his class, though he may weigh less. At present the high school weight classes (in pounds) are 98, 105, 112, 119, 126, 132, 138, 145, 155, 167, 185, and heavyweight. The intercollegiate classes include 118, 126, 134, 142, 150, 158, 167, 177, 190, and heavyweight. In the heavyweight class, the contestant must weigh a minimum of 184 pounds in high school and 177 pounds in college.

Both high-school and college matches have three periods. In high school, each period is two minutes in duration. Intercollegiate matches begin with a three-minute period followed by two two-minute periods. Thus, intercollegiate matches are one minute longer than scholastic bouts.

The match must take place on a cushioned mat whose thickness shall not be less than one which has the shock-absorbing qualities of a two-inch-thick hairfelt mat. Almost all mats presently used are of the plastic-foam type that lend themselves to easy washing and sterilization. At the high-school level, the match must take place either within a circle 28 feet in diameter or within a square 24 feet on each side. At least five linear feet of mat must surround the wrestling area itself.[1] For example, if the wrestlers are using a square, then the minimum size of the mat would be 34 feet on each side. Within a ten-foot-diameter circle in the center of the mat are two starting lines, ten inches apart (twelve inches to outside dimensions), and three feet in length. These starting lines mark the position for each wrestler when taking the referee's position (see Figure 3-1).

The match begins when both contestants meet in the ten-foot circle, shake hands, and begin wrestling on a signal from the referee. In the first period, both contestants endeavor to take their opponent down. If a fall (often referred to as a pin) occurs, the match is immediately over. A fall takes place when the points of both shoulders are held against the mat for a specified period of time—two seconds in high-school matches; one second in collegiate competition. When a wrestler is taken down, he is brought to the mat within bounds. This usually involves at least three support points—the knees (two points) and one arm. Control can occur when two support points are controlled; for instance, when the controlled wrestler has his weight on his hands and neither knee is touching the mat (wheelbarrow). The wrestler who scores a takedown is said to be "in control" of his opponent. That is, he is in a position to dominate his opponent and deny him the opportunity to move into an advantageous position. The "in control" wrestler is usually in a position where the majority of his body weight is supported by the "controlled" wrestler. Once in control, he should work to "pin" his opponent through the application of one or more pinning holds, or combination of holds, that we will learn about later. Meanwhile, the wrestler who is being controlled must continually endeavor to "escape" the controlling hold or attempt to gain control, i.e., "reverse" his opponent.

At the beginning of the second period, one of the wrestlers (determined by the flip of a coin or disc by the referee when the two captains meet before the match) will take the position of control (or advantage). In tournaments, the referee flips a disc or coin at the end of the first period of each match in order to determine which wrestler will take the control position to begin the second period. The wrestler who begins in the control (or "up") position is really in an offensive position since, on a signal from the referee to begin to wrestle, he will immediately start working for a fall. The wrestler in the offensive position is at his opponent's side, with one arm around his opponent's waist and a hand on his

[1]This requirement is for safety reasons (to protect the contestant when falling or being thrown out-of-bounds).

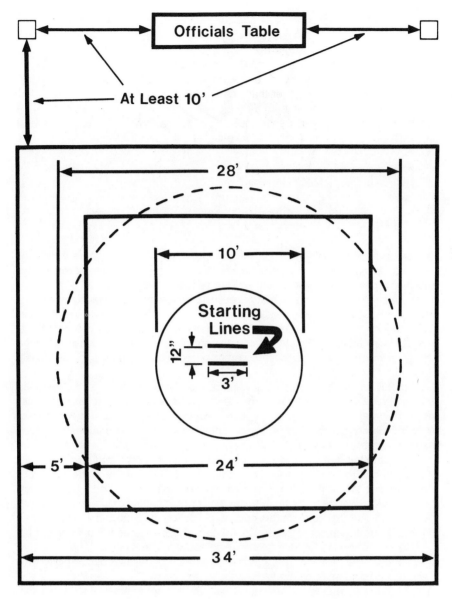

Figure 3-1 Scholastic Wrestling Mat and Mat Area

elbow.[2] In this starting position, known as the referee's position, the wrestler in the defensive (or "down") position is on his hands and knees. (See Figure 3-2 for

[2]The 1982 rules permit an optional starting position where the offensive wrestler positions himself on either side or to the rear of his opponent. He places his hands on his opponent's back with the thumbs touching. Only the hands are to be in contact with the defensive wrestler.

11

Figure 3-2 Referee's Position

an example of the referee's, or starting, position.) If no fall occurs during the second period, the third period begins with the two wrestlers reversing the positions taken at the start of the second period.

During the course of the match, each wrestler may receive points for the skillful execution of a hold that results in an escape from a controlled position, obtaining control over his opponent, or putting his opponent in a near-fall or predicament situation. Points are counted against a wrestler who uses an illegal hold, is unnecessarily rough, or commits a technical violation such as illegally locking his hands.

If no fall occurs, the wrestler having the most total points wins. If each wrestler ends the match with the same number of points, the match is declared a draw. In tournament competition, if the *regular* match ends in a draw an overtime match consisting of three one-minute periods is wrestled in order to determine a winner.

To determine the winner of an *overtime* match which ends in a tie, the following criteria are applied in the order listed. It should be understood that these criteria apply first to the overtime period and then to the regular match.

1. If a wrestler has been penalized for misconduct, abusive or unsportsmanlike conduct, his opponent shall be declared the winner.
2. If a tie remains, the wrestler who has accumulated the greater number of points for near-falls shall be declared the winner.
3. If a tie remains, the wrestler with the greater number of takedowns shall be declared the winner.
4. If a tie remains, the wrestler with the greater number of reversals shall be declared the winner.
5. If a tie remains, the wrestler with the greater number of escapes shall be declared the winner.
6. If a tie remains, the wrestler whose opponent has been penalized the greater number of times for stalling shall be declared the winner.
7. If a tie remains, the wrestler whose opponent has been warned the greater number of times for stalling shall be declared the winner.
8. If a tie remains, the wrestler who scored the first near-fall shall be declared the winner.

9. If a tie remains, the wrestler who earned the first takedown shall be declared the winner.
10. If none of the foregoing resolves the tie, the referee shall determine the winner on the basis of overall wrestling ability, including aggressiveness.

PRINCIPAL DIFFERENCES BETWEEN HIGH SCHOOL AND COLLEGIATE WRESTLING RULES

There are several differences between college and high-school rules, and fans who are not aware of them may be confused at a match. For example, someone who sees a lot of high-school wrestling may feel the official is calling falls too fast when he sees his first collegiate match. He may not realize that, to pin an opponent in a high-school match, one must hold his shoulders flat for a period of *two* seconds. In a college match, they need to be flat for only *one* second in order for a fall to take place. The reader is urged to become completely familiar with these differences in order to more fully enjoy both collegiate and scholastic wrestling.

With regard to the size of the mat itself, we have already stated that the minimum wrestling area for high-school competition is either a circle 28 feet in diameter or a square 24 feet on a side. The college wrestling area is larger—the minimum permissible size is either a circle 32 feet in diameter or a square 32 feet on a side. College regulations specify a maximum area of a square 42 feet on a side or a circle 42 feet in diameter. No mention is made in the high-school rules regarding the maximum size of mats.

College rules permit more flexibility in competition at different weights. The more restrictive rule at the high-school level tends to prevent a boy from being completely outclassed and subjected to injury because of wrestling too large an opponent. The high-school rule states that a wrestler weighing in for one weight class may be shifted to a higher weight, provided it is *not more than one* weight class above that for which his actual weight qualifies him. The college rule regarding competition weights states that a contestant who weighs in for one weight may be shifted to any higher weight class. For example, a high-school boy who weighs in at 98 pounds would not be allowed to compete that day for any weight class above 105-pounds. On the other hand, a college contestant weighing in at 118 pounds would be allowed to compete at any of the higher weight classes except unlimited, for which he must weigh at least 177 pounds.

Another major difference is the rule relating to out-of-bounds and near-fall. Many officials have been severely criticized by spectators who are not aware of this rule and how it differs at the two levels of participation. In many states, a high school wrestler can earn near-fall points or a fall only while his opponent's shoulders are within the bounds of the wrestling area. As soon as the defensive wrestler's shoulders are out-of bounds, the official will have the participants return to the center of the mat to resume competition. The college rule is quite different. It states that, when there is a pinning situation, wrestling may continue as long as *one wrestler's supporting points are in-bounds.* However, points are not awarded until the defensive participant's shoulders are within bounds.

Another situation that results in different evaluations at the two levels is when the defensive wrestler is in a pinning situation, yet supporting his torso on his elbows so that his shoulders are more than four inches from the mat. At the college level, this would be called a near-fall. Since no similar rule is in effect at the high-school level, it is very unlikely that a near-fall would be awarded in this situation. The high-school rule states that a near-fall is awarded if both shoulders are held within four inches of the mat momentarily.

Perhaps the greatest difference in the two levels is the scoring for riding advantage time. In high-school wrestling, no score is given for riding time,[3] while in college, one point is awarded to the wrestler who accrues one minute or more riding time than his opponent. It is the feeling of the authors that the high-school rule should be changed so that a point can be awarded for riding time. To ride an opponent successfully requires real skill, and we believe this should be recognized at the high-school level. Then, too, we feel it is desirable to have consistency between the high-school and the collegiate rules.

As has already been mentioned, to gain a fall it is necessary to hold both shoulders of the opponent flat against the mat for a period of two seconds in high-school wrestling, but for only one second in college wrestling. Some readers must be wondering how this brief time can be measured accurately. A skillful official does this quite easily just by counting "one thousand and one" for one second, and so on.

Finally, there are the different weight classes to which we referred previously—twelve at the high-school level and ten at the collegiate level. There is currently much talk of adding a super-heavyweight class for men over 250 pounds. At the high-school level, New York State already has a super-heavyweight class.

We will talk more about the importance of weigh-in time in Chapter 6, Weight Control and Training. There is, however, a significant difference between the two levels of competition with regard to the weigh-in before dual meets. High-school rules require that the contestants weigh in together, a maximum of one hour and a minimum of one-half hour before the scheduled dual-meeting starting time. By mutual consent of the two coaches, this thirty-minute weigh-in can precede a meet preliminary to the varsity meet (for example, a junior-varsity meet). The college rule states that weigh-ins must take place on the host team's scales a maximum of five hours and a minimum of one-half hour before the scheduled dual-meet starting time. The exact weigh-in time shall be decided by mutual agreement of the competing teams. At the present time, consideration is being given to having college teams weigh in one hour before the meet. Both teams may weigh in on their home scales by mutual agreement of the coaches.

The matter of weight allowances is also different at the two levels of competition. High schools have two rules affecting this subject, one relative to growth allowance and a second regarding tournaments. Authorities believe that it is wise to provide for normal body development and thus allow a wrestler to stay at his chosen weight the entire season. This rule allows two pounds over the wrestler's weight-class maximum beginning January 1 and one additional pound on both February 1 and March 1.

[3]A few states do give points for riding time; for example, New Jersey.

14

Figure 3-3 Restriction of Breathing   **Figure 3-4** Neck Wrench

The second rule applies to the second day of competition when a tournament runs two or more consecutive days. A one-pound allowance is permitted for the second day under such conditions. One pound is also allowed for dual meets conducted on consecutive days.

College competition permits more time for the wrestler to get to his chosen weight. Here the rule allows three pounds over the regular weight class during November and December; two pounds during January; and one pound during February. However, no allowance is given for qualifying tournaments. In those tournaments where a team is wrestling on two or three successive days, one pound per day to a maximum of two pounds is permitted.

We have already mentioned the differences in match length. High-school dual meets have three two-minute periods. In tournament consolation matches, the first period is one-minute while the second and third periods are two minutes each. In college dual meets, the first period is three minutes, followed by two two-minute periods. Consolation competition at the collegiate level requires three two-minute periods.

The two sets of rules also show differences in determining illegal holds. Readers are urged to carefully study the following rules and accompanying illustrations so that they will immediately be able to recognize an illegal hold. High-school rules address three such types of holds:

1. Any hold in which pressure is exerted over the opponent's mouth, nose, or throat that restricts breathing or circulation (see Figure 3-3).
2. Straight back salto to the head.
3. Neck wrench (Figure 3-4).

College rules state that any holds over the mouth, nose, eyes, or front of throat are potentially dangerous and are not permitted. It should be understood that there are other holds that are also considered potentially dangerous and are

a

b

Figure 3-5a Illegal Headlock   **Figure 3-5b** Full Nelson

therefore not permitted; for example, Figure 3-5 illustrates an illegal headlock (a) and an illegal full nelson (b).

Many spectators are confused about the definition of stalling when both wrestlers are in a neutral position. The high-school rules state that wrestlers must make an honest attempt to stay within the ten-foot circle and must wrestle aggressively at all times. In college wrestling, a wrestler who steps out of the ten-foot circle is cautioned immediately for stalling; it is only during contact situations that wrestlers in the neutral position may leave the ten-foot circle.[4]

A second rule applicable at the collegiate level but not at the high-school level is that the official must give a stalling warning to one of the wrestlers after the first period if no points or no warning has occurred. This rule applies to the first period in overtime competition, as well. The referee will penalize the contestant who, in his opinion, is the less aggressive wrestler. This seems to deter stalling and promote aggressiveness.

The rules pertaining to stalling while one is in the position of advantage are similar at both the collegiate and the high-school levels. Both sets of rules indicate that the wrestler in the advantage position on the mat must wrestle aggressively and attempt to secure a fall. Thus, the wrestler who is merely controlling his opponent by riding his legs would be given a "stall warning" since he is neither wrestling aggressively nor endeavoring to secure a fall.

Stalling by the wrestler in the defensive position occurs when he does not actively endeavor either to escape or to reverse his opponent. Both the college and high-school rules are consistent in their identification of defensive stalling.

When a college wrestler is injured, the injury time-out is limited to a maxi-

---

[4]This rule is not recorded in the rule book, but is shown on the official NCAA rules videotape. Most officials do enforce this rule, despite its absence from the rule book.

mum of two minutes, and coaching of the injured wrestler during the time-out is a technical violation. In high-school wrestling, however, the coach may advise his wrestler during an injury time-out, which is limited to a maximum of three minutes.

There is also a difference between high-school and college rules with regard to nosebleeds. The high-school rule does not count an injury time-out for a nosebleed. However, time required to control the bleeding from any other injury *is* counted as an injury time-out. The college rule indicates that a nosebleed or any other excessive bleeding shall be interpreted as an injury and shall be treated as an injury time-out without recording of time. The authors believe the high-school rule should be consistent with the college rule in this instance.

High-school rules restrict the number of full-length matches in which a wrestler may compete in tournament competition to four per day. In college rules, no limit is indicated.

As already mentioned, the high-school rule requires that contestants in the heavyweight class must weigh a minimum of 185 pounds; while at the collegiate level, a minimum weight of 177 pounds is specified for the heavyweight class.

Finally, at the high-school level, the use of any artificial-heat device (i.e., sweat box, hot shower, whirlpool, etc.) and the use of diuretics or other drugs for purposes of weight reduction are prohibited. A similar rule does not exist at the college level.

SIMILARITIES AND DIFFERENCES IN SCORING AT THE HIGH-SCHOOL AND COLLEGE LEVELS

In this section, we will discuss the maneuvers for which points are awarded (i.e., takedown, escape, reversal, and near-fall) and those violations for which penalty points are given (i.e., illegal holds, technical violations, and unnecessary roughness). The following list shows how individual match points are scored in collegiate competition:

Near-Fall ---2 or 3 points
Takedown --2 points
Reversal --2 points
Escape --1 point
Time advantage of one minute
    or more---1 point
Penalty points --1 to 4 points

Scholastic matches use the same method of scoring, except that points are not awarded for time advantage.

Probably the first maneuver you should be able to identify is a takedown. A wrestler is awarded a takedown when he gains control of his opponent while the supporting points of either himself or his opponent, or both himself and his opponent, are in-bounds.[5] In gaining control, he must bring his opponent down

---

[5]A wrestler's supporting points are the parts of the body bearing the wrestler's weight. When down on the mat, the usual supporting points are knees, side of thigh, or buttocks.

17

on the mat; that is, his opponent will have one or both knees touching the mat. A takedown would also occur if the defensive man's legs are controlled, but not necessarily touching the mat with either knee, and his weight is being supported by his hands. A wrestler who achieves a takedown is awarded two points.

An <u>escape</u> is usually quite easy to identify. It occurs when the offensive wrestler is no longer in control and the defensive wrestler has attained a neutral position. The wrestler who escapes is given one point.

A <u>reversal</u> takes place when the defensive wrestler comes from a position of being controlled to a position of control, while the supporting points of either wrestler are in-bounds. The reversal is worth two points.

The offensive wrestler can gain a <u>near-fall</u> when he has his opponent in a pinning situation and he either has both shoulders of his opponent stopped momentarily within four inches of the mat or has one shoulder of his opponent on the mat with the other momentarily held at an angle of 45 degrees or less. The shoulders of the opponent must be in-bounds. Only one near-fall may be awarded in a given pinning situation, so no matter how often the defensive wrestler is brought within four inches of the mat during a given hold combination, the offensive wrestler only scores once for a near-fall situation. If the near-fall situation is maintained continuously for five seconds, the offensive contestant is awarded three points. A near-fall situation of less than five seconds earns the controlling wrestler two points. Although it is not possible for the defensive wrestler to score a near-fall, it is possible for him to score a fall. For example, in a bridgeback the offensive wrestler may be pinned even though he has a controlling scissors on the defensive man.

In addition to the individual match points that can be earned, penalty points are awarded for the following rule infractions:

1. Illegal holds
2. Technical violations
3. Unnecessary roughness

Except for the technical violations of (a) assuming an incorrect starting position and (b) a false start, the wrestler who commits a foul is penalized by having his opponent receive one point for the first violation, an additional point for the second violation, two points for a third violation, and, if a fourth violation occurs, the wrestler is disqualified. The sequence of penalties for both false starts and incorrect starting positions is: (a) a visual caution from the referee, who forms a "C" with the forefinger and thumb; then (b) a penalty point. For the violation of stalling, a warning precedes the visual caution and penalty point sequence.

Although we have already pointed out the differences in the rules between college and high-school wrestling with regard to illegal holds, we have not reviewed those illegal holds where the two sets of rules are in full agreement. Examples of holds that are considered to be illegal at both levels of competition would include the following:

1. A slam is an illegal hold and occurs when one wrestler lifts his opponent and returns him to the mat with unnecessary roughness—for instance, if the defensive wrestler is brought to the mat with such force that the upper half of his body makes contact prior to the rest of his body.
2. A full straight-back suplay is an illegal hold that usually occurs when the wrestler in control is in a rear-standing position.

Figure 3-6 Twisting Hammerlock

3. A defensive wrestler can commit an illegal hold by taking a forceful fall-back from a standing position while his opponent has a cross-body or scissor ride.

4. Pulling back the thumb or any finger in order to break an opponent's hold is also considered to be an illegal hold. To be legal, at least four fingers must be grasped.

Other illegal holds common to both scholastic and collegiate wrestling include a hammerlock when the arm is pulled into a position where the angle between the lower arm and upper arm is less than 90 degrees; twisting hammerlock (see Figure 3-6); full nelson; any head lock in which the arms or hands are locked around the head of one's opponent without encircling an arm or leg (this rule does not apply to the guillotine); head scissors (see Figure 3-7); any strangle holds; twisting kneelock; bending, twisting, or forcing the head, neck, or any limb beyond what is considered its normal range of movement; and, finally, any hold applied for punishment's sake alone.

There are a number of holds that are classified as being *potentially* dangerous. When any of these holds are applied, the referee should caution the contestant against converting the potentially dangerous hold into an illegal hold. If the referee feels a potentially dangerous hold has progressed to the point where injury may occur, he should stop the hold at once. In general, a potentially dangerous hold occurs when any part of the body is forced near its maximum range of normal movement. The most common holds of this nature include: double wrist-

Figure 3-7 Head Scissors

lock, split scissors, guillotine (when the arm is pushed nearly to its maximum range of normal motion); chicken wing; toeholds; headlocks with arm or head encircled. It should be noted that both the double wristlock and the chicken wing become illegal only when the force applied is mostly parallel to the body length so that the arm is forced into a twisting hammerlock position.

The current rules enumerate ten technical violations:

1. Delay of match. Any action that results in a needless delay is considered a technical violation and would include actions such as a slow return to the center of the mat from out-of-bounds or the unnecessary altering or adjusting of one's equipment—for instance, untying and retying one's shoelaces.

2. Assuming an incorrect starting position. The correct starting positions have already been discussed. If either wrestler does not assume the correct position, he is cautioned. If the violation occurs a second time, a penalty point is awarded.

3. False start. The wrestler is given a caution the first time a false start occurs, and a penalty point is awarded for subsequent false starts.

4. Deliberately leaving the wrestling area or forcing an opponent out-of-bounds.

5. Grasping the wearing apparel, including headgear or clothing, of an opponent.

6. Interlocking or overlapping the hands around an opponent's legs or body by the wrestler in the control position. This is not allowed unless the opponent is standing or the hands are locked as part of a pinning combination. This is perhaps the technical violation that occurs most frequently, especially at the high-school level.

7. Leaving the mat without obtaining permission from the official.

8. General misconduct. This would include profanity, throwing one's headgear, expressing displeasure at a call of the official, and similar acts.

9. The figure 4 scissors is a technical violation when applied to the body or around two legs.

10. Stalling. More penalty points are awarded because of stalling than for all other infractions combined.

The technical violation of stalling is evidenced in several ways. The high-school rules state that it is stalling in the neutral position when a wrestler: "(a) continuously avoids contact with his opponent; or (b) plays the edge of the mat; or (c) prevents his opponent from returning to or remaining inbounds; or (d) initial step takes him out of the ten foot circle; or (e) is not attempting to secure a takedown."[6] The NCAA college rules indicate that stalling also occurs when repeated grasping or interlocking of hands around the leg or legs results in a stalemate or if the repeated grasping and holding of the leg or legs with both hands or arms is merely to break the defensive wrestler down or to keep him under control.

Unnecessary roughness, as one would suppose, includes any act which would be considered to have been done for punishment alone. Hairpulling, biting,

[6]Frita L. McGinness (ed.), *National Federation Edition, Wrestling Rules* (Elgin, Ill.: National Federation of State High School Associations, 1981), p. 26.

punching, scratching, kicking, and similar acts would fall in this category.

Team Scoring

Team points are based on the results of the individual matches wrestled during a meet. Individual matches end in one of eight possible ways, each of which earns from two to six team points. The eight possible outcomes of individual matches and the number of team points earned are:

1. Winning by a decision of fewer than eight points results in three team points.
2. Winning by a decision of eight to eleven points is referred to as a major decision and accounts for four team points.
3. Winning by a decision of twelve points or more is known as a superior decision and results in five team points.
4. Winning by a fall or a pin earns six team points.
5. When the number of points earned by both wrestlers is identical, a draw or tie occurs and each team is awarded two team points.
6. If one of the two wrestlers is unable to continue the match because of an injury or any other reason, the opponent is awarded a win by default, which accounts for six team points.
7. When a wrestler is not permitted to continue the match because of penalties declared by the official, the wrestler is disqualified and his opponent wins the match, garnering six team points.
8. A wrestler wins by a forfeit when, for any reason, his opponent does not appear; and six team points are awarded.

SUMMARY

Table 3-1 summarizes the similarities and differences between high-school and college wrestling rules. Although the rules and regulations discussed in this chapter are currently in effect, it must be remembered that periodically they may be modified, new ones added, or some deleted. If you become familiar with these rules and regulations, it will increase your enjoyment as a spectator since you will be better able to recognize both good wrestling and good officiating. Consequently, it will help you become a more appreciative spectator, as well, with added enthusiasm for the sport.

Table 3–1 Differences between High-School and College Wrestling Rules

PARAMETER	COLLEGIATE	SCHOLASTIC
Weights (pounds)	118, 126, 134, 142, 150, 158, 167, 177, 190, Heavyweight (> 177.)	98, 105, 112, 119, 126, 132, 138, 145, 155, 167, 185, Heavyweight (> 185.)
Length of Match	3 + 2 + 2 = 7 minutes	2 + 2 + 2 = 6 minutes
Length of Overtime Periods	1 + 1 + 1 = 3 minutes	1 + 1 + 1 = 3 minutes
Scoring (individual):	(points earned)	(points earned)
Takedown	2	2
Escape	1	1
Reversal	2	2
Near-fall	3 or 2	3 or 2
Riding time advantage	1	0
Scoring (team):		
Fall	6	6
Default	6	6
Disqualification	6	6
Forfeit	6	6
Decision (by 12 or more points)	5	5
Decision (by 8–11 points)	4	4
Decision (by less than 8 points)	3	3
Draw	2	2
Scoring (tournament):		
Fall	1	2
Default	1	2
Disqualification	1	2
Forfeit	1	2
Advancement	1, ½	2, 1
Decision (by 12 or more points)	¾	1
Decision (by 8–11 points)	½	½
Starting Position	One knee must be down	Knee or near side must be down
Time shoulders must be down for fall	1 second	2 seconds
Mat area	Minimum 32-ft. square or 32-ft. diameter circle; 5-ft. width extending around wrestling area	Minimum 24-ft. square or 28-ft. diameter circle; 5-ft. width extending around wrestling area

Table 3–1 *Continued*

Weight allowance	3 lbs. in Nov. & Dec.; 2 lbs. in Jan.; 1 lb. in Feb; no allowance for qualifying and national tounaments	2 lbs. on Dec. 25 plus 1 lb. on Feb. 1 plus 1 lb. on March 1
Weigh-in	5-hr. max. & 1-hr. min. before time of meet (usually 1 hr.)	1-hr. max. and ½-hr. min. before time of meet
Weight-class allowance	May compete at any higher weight class except unlimited, if < 177 lb	One weight class above what his actual weight qualifies
Illegal holds (where differences apply)	Any hold over the mouth, nose, or front of throat	Any hold with which pressure is exerted over the opponent's mouth, nose, or throat which restricts breathing or circulation; straight-back salto to the head; neck wrench
First-period stalling warning	Warning must be given at end of period if no points or no warning has occurred	No similar rule
Coaching of injured wrestler	Not permitted during the time-out	Permitted during the time-out
Number of full-length matches permitted per day	No rule	Four

4

Safety

May you go safe, my friend, across that dizzy way
No wider than a hair, by which your people go
From Earth to Paradise; may you go safe today
With stars and space above, and time and stars below.
—Edward John Moreton Grax Plunkett,
"May You Go Safe: On the Death
of a Muhammedan Friend"

Certainly the safety of our athletes should be everyone's concern. It is the purpose of this chapter to review some of the precautions both inside and outside the wrestling room, which should be a part of all wrestling programs in order to help assure the safety of the athlete. Although the coach is ultimately responsible for the safety of each participant in his program, both the wrestler and his parents should share this responsibility, as well.

Based on the number of accidents per thousand participants in both collegiate and scholastic body-contact sports, there has been a reduction in both the number and severity of injuries occurring. This is due primarily to the emphasis on safety by both coaching staffs and school administrators. As mentioned in Chapter 1, wrestling is currently one of the safest body-contact sports,[1] and the majority of injuries received are limited to sprains, pulls, bruises, and minor contusions.

Improvement in equipment has also contributed to the decrease in the number and severity of wrestling injuries. Perhaps the biggest advance has been in the design of wrestling mats, which have been so improved that even common mat burns have been practically eliminated. The vinyl-coated mats of today are compounded with anti-bacterial and anti-fungal agents, permit easy cleaning with mild soap and water, and can be readily disinfected, thus eliminating many skin infections such as dermatitis and herpes simplex. Their structure offers shock absorption characteristics, thus preventing injury during falls. These mats not only provide adequate cushioning, but they are sufficiently resilient to allow the athlete to rebound or spring up once he has been thrown to the mat. The old canvas-type mats were the cause of many skin infections and also had poor

---

[1]Lloyd, Deaver, and Eastwood, in *Safety in Athletics,* reported in 1959 that wrestling ranked fifth in the incidence of injuries among high-school sports.

cushioning and resiliency characteristics. The combination of cushioning (or absorption) and rebounding (or resilience) creates what is know as the "severity index" of the mat. Wrestling mats currently must have a certain severity index in order to assure that they have both the capability to absorb impact and to allow the athlete to spring back into action.

We learned in Chapter 3 that the rules in wrestling are continually being altered in order to help prevent injuries and to make the sport more appealing to the spectator and more rewarding for the wrestler. The National Federation Wrestling Rules Committee has already stated that safety is one of its primary concerns. For example, one rule now reads: "When the defensive wrestler stands, supporting all of the weight of the offensive wrestler, a potentially dangerous situation exists and the referee shall stop the match."[2]

We have developed the following list of twenty-two points to make wrestling as safe as possible, and advocate that they be included as part of a well-tailored program:

1. Have telephone communication available in an area near the wrestling room. Attending physician's (physicians') telephone number(s) should be posted in a conspicuous place near the telephone.

2. Maintain an up-to-date listing of both the home and business telephone numbers of the parents or guardians of each wrestler.

3. A well-equipped first-aid room should be maintained near the wrestling room. Minimum equipment and materials would include:
   a. gauze squares (4 × 4 inches is a good size)
   b. bandage compresses
   c. cotton
   d. roller bandage
   e. triangular bandage
   f. adhesive tape
   g. rubbing alcohol
   h. mild soap
   i. tincture of iodine or merthiolate
   j. water basin
   k. sodium chloride tablets
   l. splints suitable for arm or leg
   m. portable litter
   n. sheets, pillow, and blankets
   o. cold packs
   p. vaseline

4. An active file giving pertinent information on the health, history, and personal data of each wrestler should be maintained. This information could be kept on a 5 × 8-inch card; for example, see Figure 4-1.

5. Keep a supply of accident-record forms on hand in the wrestling room. The coach should complete the accident form in detail within 24-hours following the occurrence of any accident. Figure 4-2 illustrates the information that should be recorded.

6. A daily record of each wrestler's weight, before and after each workout, should be kept in the wrestling room adjacent to the scale. Each wrestler should post his own weight on the chart. The coach should periodically audit each wrestler's weight to be sure there has not been a dramatic increase or decline in the weight of any wrestler. A careful monitoring of each wrestler's weight is a worthwhile step toward maintaining the well-being of the entire wrestling team.

[2]This rule applies to scholastic wrestling only. See McGinness, *1981–82 National Federation Edition, Wrestling Rule Book*, p. 23.

7. It is important that only qualified officials be used during competition. A well-qualified official is knowledgeable about dangerous or potentially dangerous holds and will not permit their use, thus helping to assure the safety of the participants. The good official always remembers that any hold that endangers life or limb is completely illegal in amateur wrestling.

8. Any laceration or abrasion suffered should be treated immediately. The wrestler and his parents should assume responsibility for keeping the injury clean and watching it to be sure that infection does not occur.

9. Each wrestler should take a hot, soapy shower after each workout. This practice will not only prevent skin infections but is generally thought to combat common colds and similar respiratory and contagious infections.

10. Each wrestler should be responsible for keeping his equipment and clothing clean. This practice will discourage skin infections and the spreading of colds and respiratory diseases.

11. The coach and/or his staff should have the wrestling mats disinfected daily. Commercial disinfectants such as 20-Blue and V3 Foam Mat

---

Name _____ Date of Birth _____
Home Address _____ Home Phone _____
Parent or Guardian _____
Address of Parent or Guardian _____
Business Phone of Parent or Guardian _____ Home Phone _____
Personal Physician _____
Business Phone of Physician _____ Home Phone _____

HEALTH RECORD

Weight _____ on _____ Height _____ on _____
Certified to Wrestle at _____ Pounds, on _____
Blood Type _____ Hemophilia _____
Diabetic _____ Epileptic _____ Asthmatic _____
Allergic to Tetanus _____ Circulatory Problem _____
Eyeglass Prescription _____

RECORD OF PAST ILLNESSES

Illness   Date   Remarks

Figure 4-1   Coach's Personal Record Card

27

REPORT OF WRESTLING ACCIDENT

Name of involved participant _____

Date of accident _____ Day of week _____ Time _____

Did an injury result? _____ If yes, describe _____

Check nature of injury: Sprain _____ Strain _____ Contusion _____
                        Laceration _____ Fracture _____ Dislocation _____
                        Cauliflower Ear _____ Skin Infection _____
                        Other _____

Location of injury _____

Severity of injury _____

Was participant engaged in competition? _____

If yes, with whom _____

Age of participant _____ Weight _____ Height _____

Age of opponent _____ Weight _____ Height _____

Was a physician notified? _____ Who? _____

Was first aid administered? _____ By whom? _____

Parent or guardian of participant _____

Address of parent or guardian _____

Telephone number of parent or guardian _____

Date & time parent or guardian was notified of accident _____

Did the participant have an adequate warm-up? _____

Was the condition of the mat responsible for the accident? _____

If yes, describe _____

Was the participant's equipment responsible? _____

If yes, describe _____

Did the official, in your opinion, permit a potentially dangerous hold? _____

If yes, describe _____

How do you feel this accident could have been prevented? _____

Witness to accident _____ Telephone _____

Witness to accident _____ Telephone _____

Witness to accident _____ Telephone _____

Coach _____ Assistant Coach _____

Insurance Company _____ Telephone _____

Figure 4-2   Form for Reporting Accident

28

Cleaner are acceptable. Clean mats will help prevent impetigo, boils, herpes simplex, and similar skin infections.[3]

12. The mats should be checked at least once a year to be sure they have adequate resiliency. Old mats lose their energy-absorbing capability and do not give the wrestler the same protection from impact that a newer one will provide.

13. In the wrestling room, mats should be placed wall-to-wall on the floor and to a minimum height of five feet on all walls and posts.

14. During workouts and competition, the participants should refrain from wearing any ornament that could lead to an accident—for example, belt buckles, rings, pins, etc.

15. Wrestlers should be encouraged to keep all finger- and toenails trimmed short. A long fingernail can be torn, causing pain to its owner. Needless to say, it can also cause pain to its owner's opponent.

16. Hair should be kept reasonably short. Long hair is not only disturbing to the athlete in competition, but it can cause him needless discomfort when his opponent inadvertently pulls it during the application of certain holds.

17. During workouts the coaching staff should see that wrestlers are paired according to both size and ability. Gross mismatches in size and/or ability can be the cause of an accident.

18. Wrestlers, during both practice and competition, should wear well-designed personal protective equipment, including proper headgear, protective padding on the knees and elbows, mouth-guards, and well-fitted wrestling shoes.

19. Only wrestlers who have been certified by a competent physician as being physically acceptable should be permitted to participate in regular workouts and competition.

20. No wrestler who is ill or is recovering from an injury should be permitted to participate until he has been re-examined by a physician.

21. Before engaging in workouts, competition, or strength-development routines, the wrestler should have participated in ample warm-up exercises. With proper warm-up (usually 10–15 minutes), strenuous participation may be undertaken with little likelihood of sprains, strains, or torn muscles. Studies have shown that over one-third of the injuries in high-school wrestling occur in the first minute of competition, which suggests insufficient warm-up before beginning.[4]

22. Finally, the coach, his staff, the wrestlers, and the parents should always keep in mind that accidents are usually caused; they don't just happen. The cause is usually due to either an unsafe act or an unsafe condition. The coach can keep unsafe conditions out of the wrestling room; he can also warn against dangerous holds, horseplay, and other unsafe acts. The wrestler has a major responsibility in avoiding unsafe conditions by getting into the best possible

[3]Ignatius John Konrad, "A Study of Wrestling Injuries in High Schools Throughout Seven Midwest States" (master's thesis, Michigan State University, 1951), p. 37.

[4]American School and Community Safety Association, *Sports Safety,* Chapter 12: Wrestling, 1977.

shape. He, too, can avoid unsafe acts by using only those techniques that have been advocated by his mentors. It has been proven that injuries decrease as experience is gained by the wrestler.

The twenty-two points enumerated above will do much to make a relatively safe sport safer. No sport will ever be completely free of accidents and injuries, but coaches, participants, parents, and fans want accidents to be minimized.

NCAA RECOMMENDATIONS

The NCAA recently issued "Sports Safety Guidelines." These guidelines provide suggestions to schools concerning sound safety practices in conjunction with athletic programs. The following guidelines were reported in the September 1979 issue of "The First Aider":

NCAA EMPHASIZES SAFETY

As part of its efforts to inform the membership of developments in the field of sports medicine and player safety, the NCAA has recently re-issued a position statement entitled "Sports Safety Guidelines." These guidelines offer suggestions to NCAA members on a sound safety program. This checklist can serve as a review for those responsible for the administration of athletic programs at all levels.

Participation medical exam: Require a thorough physical examination. Keep an annual health history.

Health insurance: Each student athlete should have, by parental coverage or institutional plan, accident and health insurance.

Preseason preparation: Protect the athlete from premature exposure to the full rigors of the sport, especially through preseason conditioning, attention to heat stress, and cautious matching of players.

Acceptance of risk: "Informed consent" or "waiver of responsibility" by athletes or parents should be based on informed awareness of the risk of injury. Not only does the athlete share responsibility in preventive measures, but the athlete should appreciate the nature and significance of these measures.

Planning and supervision: Supervise and organize instruction. Instruction should include individualized attention to the refinements of skill development and conditioning. In addition, include first-aid evaluation with the instruction.

Equipment: As a result of the increase in product liability litigation, purchasers of equipment should be aware of impending as well as current safety standards being recommended by authoritative groups and utilize only known, reputable dealers. In addition, attention should be directed to the proper repair and fitting of equipment. Review the NOCSAE standards.

Facility: Periodically examine all facilities, including not only the competitive area, but also the warm-up and adjacent areas.

Emergency care: Reasonable attention to all possible preventive measures will not eliminate sport injuries. Each practice or contest should have the following: the presence or immediate availability of a person qualified and delegated to render emergency care; planned access to a physician by phone or nearby presence for prompt medical evaluation; planned access to a medical facility, including a plan for communication and transportation between the athletic site and medical facility; a thorough understanding by all affected parties, including the leadership of visiting teams, of the personnel and procedures involved.

Records: Documentation is fundamental to administration. Authoritative sports safety regulations, standards, and guidelines kept current and on file provide ready reference and understanding.

Accidents are often the result of either unsafe actions or unsafe conditions, such as wrestling without the protection of headgear or attempting to wrestle while being handicapped with a sprain suffered earlier in the week or being in poor physical condition. Invariably, a domino effect is associated with most injuries: the injury will not occur if the accident never happens; the accident will not take place unless there is an unsafe action; and the unsafe action will not occur if we maintain a safe environment with healthy, conditioned, well-trained athletes. A well-conceived wrestling program is one that seldom has a serious injury. The program is conducted in such a way that unsafe actions do not occur and, consequently, serious injuries are avoided.

FIRST AID

Prevention of unsafe acts is a major responsibility of the coach and his staff. On occasion, they will have to provide care for the injured athlete until professional medical help is obtained. It is anticipated that the coach or one of his staff will have had first aid or equivalent training. The following first-aid suggestions apply to those injuries that may occur during wrestling practice or competition. These are only a cursory overview and should not be considered as detailed enough to provide complete diagnoses and treatment. If a coach or parent has any doubts about any injury, a physician should always be consulted.

Contusions and Lacerations

A contusion or bruise usually is caused by a blow from a hard object. The cells in the muscle or bone may be crushed or bruised and purple marks on the skin surface usually appear. Lacerations or abrasions are tears in the skin resulting from cuts, mat burns, and blows by a sharp object.

In these types of injuries, if there is bleeding, the coach should endeavor to control hemorrhage by using direct pressure and a pressure bandage. Once bleeding is under control, the laceration area should be cleaned and protected so that infection does not occur. The area should then be covered with a cold pack in order to retard swelling. The injury should be monitored daily until recovery is complete.

Sprains, Dislocations, and Fractures

A sprain is an injury to a joint which involves tearing or stretching of ligaments and surrounding tissues, and is caused by a sudden twist or pull. A dislocation

31

occurs when the end of a bone slips partially or completely out of the socket of a joint. A fracture, of course, is when a bone is cracked or broken.

When the injury involves a joint (sprain or dislocation) or a possible fracture, the injured part should be splinted (thus making it immobile) and the wrestler should be transported by professional attendees to a hospital or medical-care facility with x-ray equipment and an attending physician.

Nervous System Injuries

Injuries involving any area from the skull to the lower spine may affect the central nervous system. When such an injury occurs, the wrestler should immediately be immobilized and medical help summoned. The wrestler should not be moved until professional help arrives. The best way to immobilize the neck (in case of an injury in that location) is to place sandbags or other weighted objects on either side of the head and neck—while the injured is lying on his back—in order to restrict all movements of the head.

Shock

Serious injuries to the body invariably cause shock that will depress body functions. In order to prevent shock, the injured should lie on his back with his head slightly lower than the rest of his body to assure an adequate supply of blood to the brain. Of course, if there is bleeding in the upper part of the body, the head should not be lowered until the bleeding is controlled. With shock there is a tendency for the body to chill, so normal body temperature should be maintained by covering the injured with a blanket or blankets.

LAWSUITS

Anytime an injury occurs, there is always the chance that a lawsuit could result. Some lawsuits are justified; others are not. People may initiate a lawsuit if they feel (a) their son has been wronged by improper care after being hurt, (b) there is inadequate coverage of costs, (c) there was delay in being notified of their son's injury, or (d) there was improper or inadequate advice on the part of the coach.

The coach is legally responsible for the athlete and should insure that conditions are safe. To reduce the likelihood of being sued and to present a sound defense in the event that he or his staff are sued, the following points should be observed in connection with the wrestling program:

1. Upon the occasion of every accident involving an injury, a detailed form (as shown in Figure 4-2) should be completed by the coach and signed by at least one witness within 24 hours of the occurrence of the accident.
2. A procedure for emergencies involving accidents should be established. This procedure should outline:
   a. first aid to the injured
   b. obtaining medical care
   c. follow-up on the treatment and care of the injured

    d. follow-up to identify the cause in order to minimize the possibility of a similar accident occurring.
3. A plan for supervision in the wrestling room should be established. This plan should identify the positions of the coach and the assistant coach (coaches) during competition and drills.
4. Safety rules and regulations should be established and enforced.
5. Accident insurance should be carried.
6. There should be regular inspections of facilities, including cleanliness of the wrestling mats, resiliency of the mats, and personal protective equipment (headgears, knee and elbow pads, etc.).
7. Only competent coaching personnel should be employed.
8. Parental permissions for participation and emergency medical care should be obtained from all participants.
9. Physical examinations should be required of all participants; and the attending physician, in conjunction with the coach, should establish weight classes in which the athlete is permitted to compete.
10. The overall program should be periodically audited by the school's attorney and insurance carrier.

5

The Principal Holds and Mechanical Advantage

A wise man is strong; yea, a man of knowledge increaseth strength.
—Proverbs 24:5

In general, we can classify all wrestling holds as falling under one of five càtegories. These are:
1. Takedowns
2. Breakdown—riding sequences
3. Pinning combinations
4. Reversals and counters
5. Escapes

The principal holds in each category will be discussed in this chapter, along with illustrations of how each hold is applied. There can be several variations in the application of a particular wrestling hold. One method will have both advantages and disadvantages over alternative methods. The methods described in this chapter do not necessarily represent the best or the only technique in connection with a particular hold. They are, however, those with which the authors have had success and are representative of sound techniques.

Before we discuss these holds, it is important that our readers have a clear understanding of the principle of mechanical advantage. By mechanical advantage, we mean the application of a comparatively small force ("f") acting through a long distance ("D") that produces a large force ("F") acting through a short distance ("d"). This is how the automobile jack enables you, by exerting a comparatively small force, to lift a heavy car. You have to push the jack handle or lever down many times; and, consequently, through a distance of several feet (D), you lift the heavy car but a few inches (d).

We can define mechanical advantage as being equal to the resulting force divided by the applied force:

$$\text{Mechanical advantage} = \frac{\text{Resulting force}}{\text{Applied force}}$$

The wrestler wants to maximize the mechanical advantage so that he gets a large resulting force from a much smaller applied force. The main principle the wrestler uses to provide good mechanical advantage is the lever. We can think of a lever as being a rigid bar (a portion of the leg or arm) free to turn on some fixed point or axis, which is called the fulcrum. The point of the fulcrum is usually established by the wrestler applying the hold. Levers may be classified in three groups, according to the relative position of the fulcrum, the applied force, and the resistance to be overcome. The relative efficiencies of these three groups should be apparent from studying the diagrams shown in Figure 5-1. The longer the distance (D) from the fulcrum to the input force (f) compared with the distance (d) from the fulcrum to the output force (F), the more efficient is the lever. Consequently, in Figure 5-1 the second-class lever is the most efficient and the third-class lever is the least efficient. Now look at Figure 5-2, which illustrates a third-class anatomical lever, consisting of the arm bones. If the hand is being pulled down with some force (F), it will take a large effort ($\frac{d}{D}$ F) for the brachialis muscle to hold the hand in the nearly horizonal position shown.

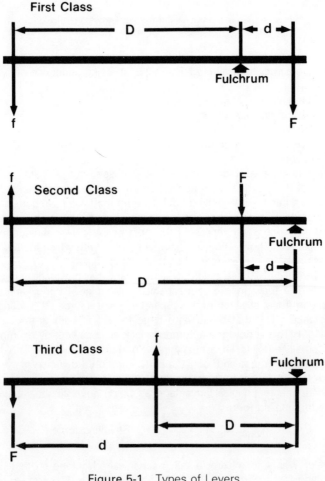

Figure 5-1   Types of Levers

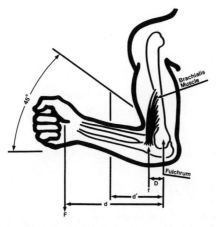

Figure 5-2 Third-class Anatomical Lever

Let us refer once again to Figure 5-1, noting that Fd = fD and that efficiency equals the output force (F) divided by the input force (f). Therefore, efficiency is $\frac{F}{f}$ = $\frac{D}{d}$. The efficiency of the second-class lever is higher since the ratio of $\frac{D}{d}$ is greater than for the first-class lever. The third-class lever has the poorest efficiency, which always will be equal to less than one. In Figure 5-2,[1] it is apparent that it would be quite difficult for the brachialis muscle to handle a force of, say, 50 pounds pushing down on the hand when the hand is in the position shown. However, if the forearm is moved to a 45 degree angle, d will be reduced to d¹, thus requiring only a load of $50\frac{d^1}{D}$ by the brachialis muscle instead of $50\frac{d}{D}$.

One more principle will be helpful in understanding mechanical advantage in wrestling. The bending moment is the product of a force and its perpendicular distance from an axis. In Figure 5-3(a) the man is lifting a 150-pound weight (for example, a 150-pound wrestler off the mat). Note that the center of this weight is only 8 inches from the joints of the lumbar spine. This load will produce a

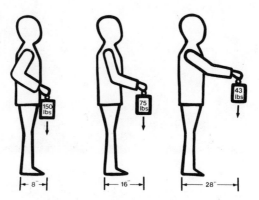

Figure 5-3 Bending Moment Principle

[1]Based on data from Institute of Rehabilitation Medicine, New York University Medical Center, New York, N.Y.

37

bending moment of 1200 inch-pounds on the sacro-lumbar joint:
$$M = (8)(150) = 1200 \text{ inch-pounds}$$

If the arms are extended so that the distance between the center of the weight lifted and the joints of the lumbar spine is 16 inches, then only a 75-pound weight can be lifted to produce the same bending moment on the sacro-lumbar joint. When the distance is extended to 28 inches, only 42.9 pounds can be lifted to produce the same bending moment. This "moment principle" is the reason you should keep any weight you lift very close to the body without having the arms extended. The wrestler, in applying various holds, takes advantage of the fundamental laws of physics.

TAKEDOWNS

The takedown maneuver is probably the most important of the five categories of holds to the amateur wrestler. Most every championship wrestler is inevitably a "takedown artist." There is a significant correlation between the wrestler who obtains the first takedown and the ultimate winner of the match. The successful takedown does not involve just one hold or one aggressive motion. It usually includes "setting up the opponent" by making a fake motion or shifting one's weight or giving the opponent a push or pull. This "setting up" sequence is rhythmically followed by one of several maneuvers.

Before we discuss specific takedown moves, let us look at three basics that should be mastered in order to achieve the desired takedown.

Stances In wrestling there are two basic stances. A square stance is one in which both feet are parallel, and a staggered stance is one in which one foot is

Figure 5-4 Stances

38

Figure 5-5   Collar-and-Elbow Tie-up

slightly ahead of the other (see Figure 5-4). As a wrestler develops his skills, he will generally choose the stance which he feels is more comfortable. Regardless of which stance a wrestler chooses, the following points should be kept in mind in order to execute both offensive and defensive moves successfully: (1) the back should be fairly straight; (2) the head should be held up; (3) the knees should be slightly bent; (4) the hands should be held in front; (5) the elbows should be held close to the body; (6) the body weight should be distributed on both feet; (7) one should not drop back on the heels of the feet; and (8) when using the staggered stance, more of the body weight should be centered over the rear foot in order to use that foot as a pushing-off point for penetration.

Setting Up   The purpose of setting up is to get a reaction from one's opponent, thus leading to a counter-offensive move. The principal setting-up methods include a body motion, a head fake, or a tie-up. There are several tie-ups used in wrestling, of which four are the most common.

The most-used tie-up is referred to as a collar-and-elbow, because one hand is placed behind the opponent's neck while the other controls his elbow (see Figure 5-5).

The second tie-up is called a collar-and-wrist tie-up, since the opponent's wrist is controlled rather than his elbow (see Figure 5-6).

A third tie-up is known as an underhook-and-wrist. The offensive wrestler reaches under the opponent's arm and puts his hand on top of his opponent's shoulder. With his other hand, he controls the opponent's wrist (see Figure 5-7).

The fourth, and perhaps most advantageous, tie-up is the collar-and-inside-arm. This is a combination of two of the preceding tie-ups, where the offensive wrestler places one hand on the opponent's neck and places his other hand on

Figure 5-6   Collar-and-Wrist Tie-up

the inside of the opponent's arm (see Figure 5-8).

In using any of the tie-ups, it is important that a comfortable stance be maintained, thus providing the opportunity for quick, maneuverable, aggressive motions as well as stability and the application of defensive combinations.

Figure 5-7   Underhook-and-Wrist Tie-up

Figure 5-8   Collar-and-Inside-Arm Tie-up

Penetration The third basic principle the wrestler should master in order to get a takedown is penetration; that is, he must quickly shorten the distance between himself and his opponent. In our experience, the wrestler who is able to get deep penetration can usually get the takedown. It is this penetration which enables one to lift his opponent. This relates to a fundamental law of physics, as illustrated in Figure 5-3.

All the takedowns described assume that the wrestler has developed a good stance, is knowledgeable in the execution of setting up his opponent, and is able to penetrate the distance to his opponent.

Single-Leg

The single-leg takedown (see Figure 5-9) is what is often referred to as a percentage takedown; that is, a higher percentage of the takedowns seen in the wrestling will be by a single-leg pick-up. There are several alternative ways to execute the single-leg move. The one described here relates to the upper single-leg, where the offensive wrestler lowers his hips while bending his knees so as to create the shortest distance between himself and the point he wants to attack. He then taks a deep penetration step, driving his head into the ribs of his opponent while grasping the near leg with both arms at or above the knee of the leg being attacked. The leg is hugged with both arms, while the offensive wrestler keeps his body tight to his opponent's knee and his head to the inside of his opponent's leg. As the leg is brought up off the mat, the outside arm should slide inward allowing the locked hands to move around to the inner side of the opponent's leg. This brings the opponent's leg up tight to the chest. The head should be tucked on the inside of the opponent's thigh. In order to secure the takedown, the offensive wrestler must now take his opponent to the mat. There are a variety of ways this can be done. One method used is to kick his opponent's non-controlled leg as he hops on this leg to try and maintain balance. This force to the leg will usually cause the defensive wrestler to go to the mat. Another technique as illustrated is to circle the opponent to the mat. This is done

Figure 5-9 Single-Leg Takedown

a

b

Figure 5-9 Continued.

c

d

by stepping the outside leg back and moving in a circle while applying pressure to the opponent's thigh with the head and to his knee with the arms and chest.

The single-leg pick-up is an efficient takedown, since it is representative of a second-class lever. The hip joint of the controlled leg acts as a fulcrum, while the leg from the hip joint to the knee is the lever arm. The input force is the lifting

Figure 5-10 Double-Leg Takedown

a

b

Figure 5-10 Continued

c

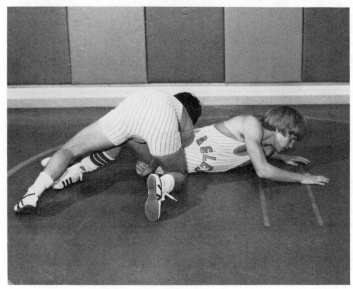

d

force applied by the two arms that lift the opponent's leg. It can be seen that it takes a relatively small input force, in view of the long lever arm, to overcome the resistance of the opponent, who endeavors to keep his leg planted on the mat.

Double-Leg

The double-leg takedown (Figure 5-10) is also a high-percentage maneuver. When executing the double-leg, the offensive wrestler bends his knees while lowering his hips and takes a deep penetration step towards his opponent, placing one foot between the opponent's feet, with his head on the outside of the opponent's body. The offensive wrestler then drives the knee of his lead leg to the mat while simultaneously stepping forward with his other leg. This deep penetration step enables the offensive wrestler to grasp both legs of his opponent at his upper thighs and to lock hands. He should keep his head up and his back nearly straight as he now lifts and spins his opponent to the mat for the takedown. It is essential that the offensive wrestler keep his opponent's body as close to the centerline of his own body as he can so as to maximize his lifting capability.

Duck-Under

A good takedown maneuver for the beginning wrestler to learn, the duck-under (see Figure 5-11) is from a collar-and-elbow tie-up. It can also be used from other tie-ups, but will be described here from the collar-and-elbow position. The offensive wrestler bends his knees while lowering his hips and takes a deep penetration step to the side of his opponent that he is going to duck under. As the offensive wrestler ducks under his opponent's arm, he moves his arm from the collar tie-up position to a position just above his opponent's elbow, thus securing the arm. The offensive wrestler then spins behind his opponent, while lifting him up and bringing him to the mat for the takedown. Again, it is important to keep the body of the opponent close to your own so as to maximize your lifting power.

Snapdown

This takedown (see Figure 5-12) is used more in scholastic than in collegiate wrestling because it is not as effective against an experienced wrestler. The snapdown can be executed best from a collar-and-elbow tie-up while the defensive wrestler is on one or both knees. The offensive wrestler initiates the maneuver by pushing forward slightly against his opponent's shoulder. This will stimulate the defensive wrestler to resist the force by pushing forward. The offensive wrestler then pulls forward with his hand, which has been placed on the back of his opponent's head, and also pulls forward with his left hand, which has grasped his opponent's upper arm. This simultaneous jerk often will pull the defensive wrestler to the mat on all fours. The offensive wrestler then closes the gap between him and his opponent by spinning behind his opponent to a controlling position.

46

Figure 5-11 Duck-Under Takedown

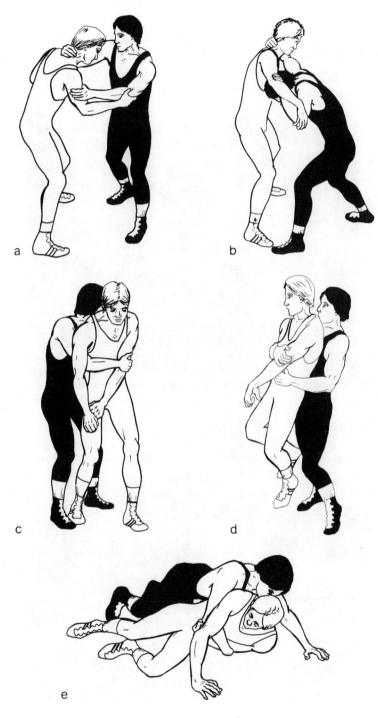

a

b

c

d

e

Fireman's Carry

The fireman's carry (Figure 5-13) can most effectively be done from an elbow-and-collar tie-up position. The offensive wrestler takes a deep step between his opponent's legs while pulling his elbow in tight. While this movement is being

Figure 5-12 Snapdown

a

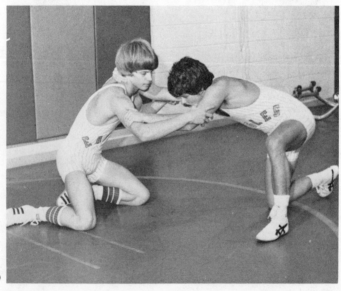

b

Figure 5-12 Continued

c

d

made, the offensive wrestler's arm which was on his opponent's neck is placed in his opponent's crotch. At this point, the center of gravity of the offensive wrestler is almost directly in line with the center of gravity of the defensive wrestler. This permits good lifting efficiency as discussed earlier. The offensive wrestler then drops to his outside hip and throws his opponent to his side. Now,

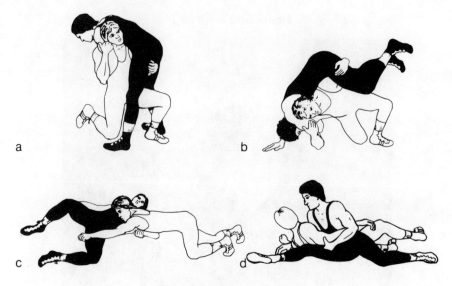

a

b

c

d

Figure 5-13 Fireman's Carry

the offensive wrestler moves his body into a control position with his arm across his opponent's chest. It is most important for beginning wrestlers to control the elbow. As long as the elbow is controlled, the maneuver may be completed in a variety of ways.

Cross-Ankle Pick

This takedown maneuver (see Figure 5-14) is a specialty execution having more application at the scholastic level where the defensive wrestler has limited experience. It is a good example of the application of a long lever arm. Although the cross-ankle pick can be executed from all of the tie-up positions, it will be described here as beginning from the elbow-and-collar tie-up. The offensive wrestler sets up his opponent by pulling him forward while simultaneously dropping to one knee. The hand that had been on the opponent's elbow now grasps his heel as he is drawn forward. While the heel is pulled up, the opponent's neck should be pulled down with the other hand, forcing the defensive wrestler to go to the mat. The offensive wrestler makes three simultaneous motions which, when performed in unison, make this maneuver successful. He pulls up on the heel with one hand while pulling down on the neck with the other hand and driving the body of the defensive wrestler back with the forearm that is next to the defensive wrestler's chest.

High-Crotch

From a collar-and-elbow tie-up, the offensive wrestler bends his knees while lowering his hips and takes a deep step toward the middle of his opponent's legs while lifting up on the elbow. The offensive wrestler drops to one knee and places his free arm high in his opponent's crotch. The opponent will react by

50

sprawling. As he does so, the offensive wrestler will pivot on his knee, drop to his outside knee, and bring his free arm back through his opponent's crotch, assuming a control position (see Figure 5-15).

Summary—Takedown Maneuvers

Many excellent takedown maneuvers have not been covered in this section and many additional refinements of the takedowns discussed will be stressed by the wrestler's coach. Only the principal takedowns have been covered here, since, if these fundamental holds are learned well, the amateur wrestler should be well on his way to a successful career.

Two points need to be reiterated. First, it is better to know a few fundamental holds in detail and be able to execute them effectively than to be able to execute a great many poorly. Second, the successful wrestler should be able to initiate holds in a rhythmic sequence. One hold that fails should blend into a second and a third and ultimately into one that proves successful. It is this smooth, never-ending sequence of maneuvers that distinguishes the really skilled wrestler.

BREAKDOWN—RIDING SEQUENCES

As we have already learned, in scholastic wrestling *no* points are earned for time advantage and in collegiate wrestling only one point can be given for a time advantage of one minute or more. However, riding is a very important maneuver for the following reasons:

1. It puts the offensive wrestler in a better position to apply a pinning hold.
2. It utilizes less energy than being ridden, and thus the relative strength and stamina of the wrestler who is riding continues to increase.
3. When overtime matches end in draws with no points awarded and the criteria listed on page 00 have not resulted in an obvious winner,

a   b

Figure 5-14 Cross-Ankle Pick

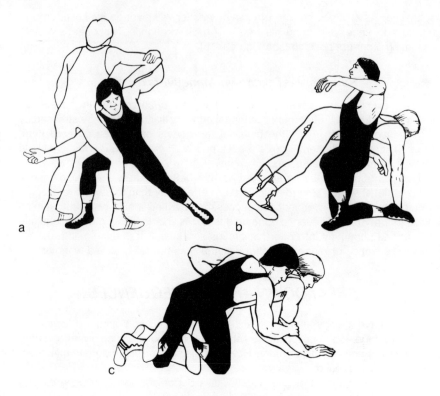

Figure 5-15 High-Crotch

then the wrestler with the greatest amount of riding time is more
likely to be declared the winner by the referee.
Of the three points mentioned above, perhaps the second one is the most
important. If a wrestler is broken down for an extended period, perhaps one
minute or more, much of his stamina will become depleted and he will be much
easier to pin, which is, of course, the wrestler's primary goal.

Top Position It is important that the offensive wrestler be in a legal starting
position (see Figure 3-2) in order to avoid a possible penalty point. From the
signal by the referee, there should be a progression by the offensive wrestler
from the top position. This progression includes: breaking one's opponent down,
riding, and applying a pinning maneuver. Of course if a pinning hold can be
applied without riding, this is desirable. From the top position, the offensive
wrestler places one arm around his opponent's waist with his other hand on the
opponent's elbow. The offensive wrestler should have his head centered in the
middle of his opponent's back.

Breakdowns

The wrestler who is in the bottom position has a base involving four points of
support (two hands and two knees). As soon as one of these points is removed,

his base is substantially weakened. These points of support are frequently referred to as "props." The wrestler in the top position should continually keep two things in mind: (1) remove one of the four props of his opponent, and (2) keep the majority of his weight in such a position that it will need to be overcome by any maneuver of his opponent. The wrestler in the top position should

a

b

Figure 5-16   Near-Arm Chop

be "pesky" in attacking the points of support of his opponent. He will attack one point, then another, never allowing his opponent to gain real stability. Removing one of the defensive wrestler's four props will put him in a vulnerable position, because the three remaining props will not be 120 degrees apart (the desirable spacing of a three-point support). In fact, two of the props will probably be less than 90 degrees apart, thus making it easier to put the defensive wrestler flat on the mat for a pin.

Near-Arm Chop This is perhaps the most common breakdown in wrestling.

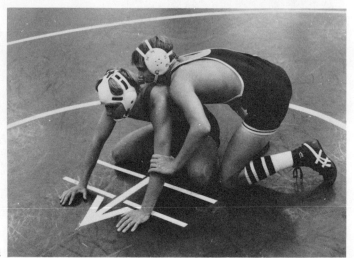

a

b

Figure 5-17 Outside-Ankle Pick

From the referee's (or starting) position, the top man lifts his arm slightly off the elbow and chops his opponent's arm in toward his body. The top man then drives downward and toward the prop that has just been removed. The top man should keep his hips in tight to his opponent at all times, thus maximizing his weight over his opponent's torso (see Figure 5-16).

Outside-Ankle Pick From the referee's position, the top man drops his arm from his opponent's waist to the shoestrings of his opponent's outside ankle. Simultaneously, he moves his other hand off the elbow of his opponent and puts his arm around his opponent's waist. After the defensive wrestler's ankle has been grasped, his entire leg is raised off the mat while the offensive wrestler drives forward. The offensive wrestler should keep his head up and his weight on the bottom man (see Figure 5-17).

Inside-Ankle Pick This breakdown is similar to the outside-ankle pick. There are situations where the top wrestler will find it advantageous to pick up the inside ankle and remove this point of support. From the referee's position, the offensive wrestler's hand will drop from his opponent's elbow to the shoelaces of the defensive wrestler's inside ankle. As the offensive wrestler lifts on the ankle, he will rise from his knees while driving forward, forcing the defensive wrestler flat on the mat (see Figure 5-18).

Rides

In all rides, the offensive wrestler should be fatiguing the defensive wrestler at a faster rate than the offensive wrestler himself is tiring. When riding an opponent, it is important that the offensive wrestler keep the majority of his weight and pressure toward the prop that has been broken down. This will result in a high "moment" for the defensive wrestler to overcome in order to regain his four-point base.

Figure 5-18 Inside-Ankle Pick

Figure 5-19 Two-on-One Ride

Two-on-One Ride When executing the two-on-one ride, the offensive wrestler moves his arm from his opponent's waist to his inside wrist. The top man will now have both of his hands on his opponent's inside arm. The offensive wrestler will keep much of his weight directly over his opponent and will execute pressure on the shoulder of the arm that is controlled while driving forward (see Figure 5-19).

Figure 5-20 Tight-Waist Ride

a

b

c

Figure 5-21 Navy Ride

57

Tight-Waist Ride The tight-waist ride is one of the most effective rides used in wrestling. To begin this ride, the offensive wrestler uses a near-arm chop, as discussed earlier. At the same time, he squeezes the waist of his opponent with the arm that is encircling it. As the offensive wrestler rides his opponent, he will continually direct body force toward his opponent's prop that has been secured (see Figure 5-20).

Navy Ride This ride is most easily executed from the outside-ankle breakdown. After the offensive wrestler has broken his opponent down to the mat, he lifts the outside leg of his opponent off the mat, reaches over the outside leg, and places his right arm between his opponent's legs at the upper thigh. This is done while his left arm encircles his opponent's waist. As the ride continues, the offensive wrestler seeks alternative props to remove (see Figure 5-21).

Chicken-Wing Ride As in most rides, the opponent must be broken down before the offensive wrestler can apply the chicken wing. He starts the chicken wing by inserting his left arm under the opponent's near forearm and over the shoulder blade (scapula). The right arm continues to be wrapped around the opponent's waist while the weight and pressure is directed toward the prop that has been controlled (see Figure 5-22).

Arm-Bar and Underhook Ride This ride is most effective since it frequently can lead to back points and/or a fall, as will be discussed later. In initiating this ride, the offensive wrestler controls his opponent's near arm by placing his outside arm under the opponent's near arm above the elbow and then across his back. The opponent's near arm is now barred. His other arm is hooked by the offensive wrestler at the armpit with the offensive wrestler's free arm.

Figure 5-22 Chicken-Wing Ride

58

Figure 5-23 Arm-Bar and Underhook Ride.

During this entire maneuver the defensive wrestler is carrying the weight of his opponent. This ride is often applied when the defensive wrestler has been broken down and endeavors to push up from his stomach (see Figure 5-23).

Cross-Body Ride This is an effective leg ride that is easily applied and can often lead to a pinning combination. The top wrestler gets a grapevine with his left leg on his opponent's left leg. This involves inserting the outside leg between the opponent's legs and hooking the foot on the opponent's inside ankle. The top man then rotates his body across his opponent's back. He should keep his hips in close to his opponent. The offensive wrestler's left arm now hooks under his opponent's ribs and is ready to catch the arm of the opponent or go inside his crotch (see Figure 5-24).

PINNING COMBINATIONS

The objective of every aggressive wrestler is to win by a fall. The usual sequence that leads to a fall is: (1) gaining control by taking an opponent down or by reversing him; (2) breaking the opponent down, followed by an energy-consuming ride; and (3) application of a pinning combination.

Generally, you must have your opponent broken down or at least off his four-point base before you will be able to effectively apply a pinning combination. The pinning combinations that will be discussed are based on the premise that the defensive wrestler is being controlled and has been broken down or taken off his base.

a

b

c

Figure 5-24 Cross-Body Ride

60

a

b

c

Figure 5-25 Half Nelson

a

b

c

Figure 5-26 Near-Side Cradle

Figure 5-26 Continued

d

e

Half Nelson

A large percentage of falls are the result of the half nelson. To achieve this pinning hold, the offensive wrestler moves his body to the side of his opponent so that he is more perpendicular than parallel to his opponent's torso. An arm is inserted underneath the opponent's armpit and the hand is placed on the back of the opponent's neck, which now becomes the fulcrum of a relatively long movement-arm (from the hand to the elbow). The farther the arm of the offensive wrestler can be inserted, the greater will be the leverage. By driving one's arm to its full length and wrapping the wrist and hand around the opponent's neck, maximum leverage can be obtained. The offensive wrestler now drives his chest against his opponent's shoulder and upper arm to turn his opponent on his back. In securing the fall, the elbow should be deep around the opponent's neck and lifting the head up while forcing the shoulders down. The offensive wrestler should support his torso on his toes so that his weight is directed toward his opponent's chest (see Figure 5-25).

Figure 5-27 Guillotine

a

b

Figure 5-27 Continued

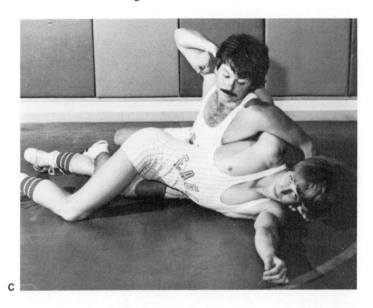

c

d

Near-Side Cradle

The near-side cradle is used as much as the half nelson. The near-arm chop breakdown is representative of what can be used to set up this important pinning hold. The removal of an opponent's prop frequently will cause him to lower his head, thus causing the distance to be shortened between his knee and head. As soon as this happens, there is an excellent opportunity for a near-side cradle. When the opponent's head is down, the offensive wrestler will apply pressure to bring the head closer to the knee. This pressure should be applied with the forearm on top of the neck. The hand should slide down across the chest of the opponent. Meanwhile, the other arm will move from the opponent's waist to his near leg. The two hands are now grasped together, locking the opponent's head and near leg close together. In order to put his opponent on his back, the offensive wrestler should drop his head to the rib cage of his opponent and drive hard. If more pressure is needed, step the rear leg up and use it to drive. Once the opponent is on his back, the lock should be secure with the offensive wrestler covering the face and neck areas. By dropping his own hip, the offensive wrestler's weight will help to hold the opponent down once he is on his back (see Figure 5-26).

Guillotine

The guillotine is a common and effective method of executing a pinning combination from the cross-body ride. From this ride, the offensive wrestler takes his arm, which has been on his opponent's ribs, and hooks the far arm of his opponent at the elbow. The offensive wrestler then secures the wrist of his opponent, using his free hand. This maneuver results in the opponent's shoulder becoming the fulcrum, with combined input forces resulting from the offensive wrestler lifting up with both arms. The lever arm is relatively long, being the distance from the wrist to the shoulder of the defensive wrestler. Thus, the mechanical advantage of this hold is high. To assist in turning the defensive wrestler over on his back, the offensive wrestler will lift his head, which had been placed under his opponent's elbow, while straightening his own back. As soon as the opponent moves toward him back, the offensive wrestler will rotate his body toward his opponent's and place the arm which was hooked on the opponent's elbow around his head. The wrist that had been secured is released so that the offensive wrestler can lock his arms and pull his opponent's head toward his, thus consumating the pin (see Figure 5-27).

Arm-Bar and Underhook

From the arm-bar and underhook ride, as discussed earlier, the offensive wrestler should continue this maneuver in an effort to gain a fall. The procedure is for the offensive wrestler to step up with his outside leg resulting in the further trapping of his opponent's arm that has been barred. Meanwhile, he keeps his far arm underhooked at the armpit of his opponent. He now walks around his opponent's head, thus forcing his opponent's shoulders to the mat. The offensive wrestler completes the maneuver in a sit-up position, while controlling both arms of his opponent (see Figure 5-28).

REVERSALS and COUNTERS

Our fourth category of holds can be referred to as reversals and counters. A

a

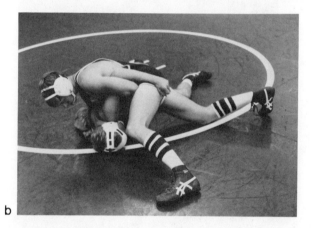

b

c

Figure 5-28 Arm-Bar and Underhook

Figure 5-29 Outside Switch

a

b

Figure 5-29 Continued

c

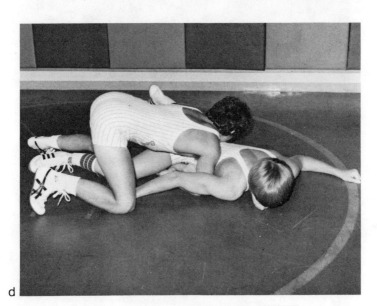

d

counter-move can be initiated for every offensive hold, while the majority of reversals—as well as escapes (which we will discuss shortly)—take place from the bottom position. You will recall that reversing one's opponent results in two points being awarded. To initiate a reversal, the bottom wrestler must try to maintain a four-point base. He will not want to surrender any of his props to the opponent.

Outside Switch

The switch is one of the most common and popular reversal maneuvers. It is a

Figure 5-30 Peterson Roll

a

b

Figure 5-30 Continued

c

d

move that can be used from several different positions and is dependent upon the proper application of the simple lever, as is characteristic of most wrestling holds. In initiating the outside switch, the bottom man begins his maneuver by snapping his inside arm to the outside. He then lifts his outside knee and sits on his outside buttock as his outside hand reaches for his opponent's inside thigh,

Figure 5-31 Hip Roll

a

b

Figure 5-31 Continued

c

d

entrapping his opponent's arm. He is now in a favorable position to take advantage of the lever principle on the trapped arm. He scoots his own hip out, causing his opponent to break down from his base. The bottom man will now move behind his opponent and place his free hand in his opponent's crotch from the back, thus completing the outside switch (see Figure 5-29).

Peterson Roll

This is a popular move because, from this maneuver, the bottom man can not only score a reversal but may pick up back points and possibly secure a fall. From the referee's (starting) position, the bottom man sits back toward his inside hip so as to be in a sitting position on the mat. From this position, the bottom man does a quick turn-in and pulls up on his controlled wrist. As the top man starts to follow behind his opponent, the bottom man puts his hand inside his opponent's knees and rolls off his right hip. As he rolls over, he hooks the leg of his opponent with his hand while keeping control of his opponent's wrist, which is still around his waist. The man who was on the bottom is now in control and is in a good position to garner back points (see Figure 5-30).

Hip Roll

The hip roll is frequently called other names, including regular roll, side roll, wrist roll, and so on. In its execution, the bottom man first gains control of his opponent's wrist, which is around his waist. He then drops to his outside hip and shoulder. The legs are bent. The upper foot now hooks the opponent's thigh, which is then elevated while the bottom man slides his lower leg straight out on the mat. This enables the bottom man to get his opponent on his side. The bottom man still maintains control of his opponent's wrist. As the opponent is raised over the bottom wrestler's body to the mat, the bottom wrestler will lift his hips and "hip-heist" the elevator leg out to finish perpendicular to the bottom man's body (see Figure 5-31).

The hip roll can be executed from several different positions, but is especially effective when one's opponent is riding at the midpoint of the back or higher. A common way of using the hip roll is after a short sit-and-turn.

Cross-Face

The cross-face is one of two counters or blocks included in this discussion. It involves the application of force with the forearm across the opponent's face, forcing his head away from the defensive man's body. This aspect of wrestling is not nearly as visible as a well-executed takedown or escape, but certainly is important in the repertoire of moves that every successful wrestler must master. A well-executed counter can act as a set-up for a succeeding offensive move.

The cross-face is a defensive maneuver that is frequently used when one's opponent has shot for a double-leg takedown. In this case, the procedure is to first sprawl by spreading the legs while throwing the feet back. In this sprawled position, it is quite difficult for the opponent to pick up the legs and gain control. From the sprawled position, the defensive wrestler will use one of his hands to peel his opponent's hand from his body by pushing down on it. Simultaneously, using the other forearm, pressure will be placed across the opponent's face. This force against the opponent's head will move his head away from the defensive man's body and enable the defensive wrestler to counter the double-leg move (see Figure 5-32).

Figure 5-32 Cross-Face

Whizzer

The whizzer may be thought of as a defensive hold used to counter almost any frontal attack. Here, we will describe its use to counter the single-leg takedown. The defensive maneuver is to sprawl with the feet well apart and the legs back, while driving the hips into the offensive wrestler. From this position, the arm that is around the outside of the defensive wrestler's leg is overhooked. This arm should be hooked above the opponent's elbow. Pressure will be applied in a downward direction on the offensive wrestler's shoulders. As this is done, the defensive wrestler steps up with his outside leg while rotating his hips so that he is now facing his opponent. The free hand of the defensive wrestler can be used to push down on the opponent's head as the hips are rotated, resulting in the securing of a neutral position (see Figure 5-33).

a   b

Figure 5-33 Whizzer

ESCAPES

Next to takedowns, escapes represent the most important class of holds. You must be in a neutral position in order to gain a takedown, so an escape (one point) followed by a takedown maneuver (two points) represents a three-point

Figure 5-34 Stand-Up

a

b

Figure 5-34 Continued

c

d

combination. The wrestler who is an escape artist will seldom get into a predicament situation or get pinned. Thus, if he can become really proficient in escaping and taking his opponent down, his success as a wrestler is assured.

Stand-Up

Although most escape holds can be executed from both a standing position and the referee's position, for the most part they are more effectively executed

Figure 5-35 Sit and Turn-In

a

b

Figure 5-35 Continued

c

d

from the standing position. In this position, the advantage wrestler has already lost some of his advantage. He no longer is able to apply the static weight of his body on top of his opponent. He no longer has the position control of his legs that he had when in the referee's position. Usually, the first maneuver that the controlled wrestler should endeavor is to stand from the referee's position. To do this and avoid being broken down requires a combination of balance, strength, and quickness.

In beginning the stand-up escape, the bottom wrestler uses his inside leg to begin his rise. At the same time, he raises his inside arm high while keeping his back straight and his head up. The defensive wrestler uses his outside arm to secure the hand that is around his waist. At the same time, he brings his inside arm down so that both of his hands are available to break his opponent's grip around his waist. To do this, he should grasp his opponent's right hand, near the thumb, with his own right hand and his opponent's left hand, near the thumb, with his own left hand. He should then push down and away from the center of his body. More force can be exerted by pushing down than pulling up, so the defensive wrestler will have some mechanical advantage over his opponent. Once the opponent's grip is broken, the defensive wrestler can step back, lower his inside shoulder, and pivot to a neutral position (see Figure 5-34).

Sit and Turn-In

From the referee's position, the bottom wrestler rotates his hips so as to be in a sitting position. Meanwhile, by keeping his elbows in, he controls the arm that is around his waist. It is usually a good idea to pull the hand of this arm up toward his chest. It is important that the bottom man not let his hips get extended away from the top man. The elbow of the bottom wrestler's other arm should be held close to his body. To turn in for an escape, the bottom wrestler will kick his outside leg high while dropping his inside shoulder to the mat and pulling up on the controlled wrist as he turns in. The bottom wrestler is now in a tripod position. If the opponent does not follow the offensive wrestler, the two wrestlers will be in a neutral position. If the opponent does follow, then the bottom wrestler will be in a good position to initiate a roll maneuver; for example, Peterson, side, wrist, etc. (see Figure 5-35).

SUMMARY

In this chapter we classified all wrestling holds in one of five categories: takedowns, breakdown-riding sequences, pinning combinations, reversals and counters, and escapes. In each category, we have selected percentage maneuvers; that is, those that have been proven to have a reasonably high probability of success.

No attempt has been made to cover all the maneuvers and holds that are part of the repertoire of championship wrestlers. To do this would require a formidable text in itself. However, if the novice and experienced wrestler can effectively execute the holds described in this chapter, he will be on his way toward becoming a skilled wrestler.

At this point, we want to emphasize that the only way to learn wrestling maneuvers is to get on a mat and work with them. They will not be learned by reading about how they should be performed or by watching skilled wrestlers perform them. It is only by continued practice that they will be learned to the extent that they can be applied with skill.

Finally, we would like to stress how important the sense of "touch" or "feel" is to the sport of wrestling. It is this touch that the experienced wrestler develops that allows him to select one maneuver after another in a smooth, rhythmic sequence. He will feel how his opponent's weight and body position is distributed in relation to his own. This dimension of "feel" is what signals the wrestler's mind to choose one maneuver over another during the course of a match.

6

Weight Control and Training

He that wrestles with us strengthens our nerves and sharpens our skill.
Our antagonist is our helper.

—Edmund Burke,
"Reflections on the Revolution
in France" (1790)

To be effective, the successful wrestler must enter each match in superb condition; and he should be wrestling at a weight that is optimum from the standpoint of strength application and energy utilization during the entire contest. "At what weight should I participate?" is a question posed by most beginning wrestlers. Weight control and the necessity for wrestlers to lose weight is perhaps one of the least understood areas of collegiate and high-school wrestling.[1]

SELECTING A WEIGHT

It is not necessary for a wrestler to miss meals, starve himself, or go on crash diets to be on the wrestling team or to be a good wrestler. We feel many parents, fans, and athletes misunderstand the concept of how a wrestler maintains an optimum weight or makes a competitive weight class. Because of such misunderstandings, the sport of wrestling has been judged unfairly by some. In order to cope with this problem, perhaps coaches should set up annual meetings to which parents, school officials, and the coaching staff are invited in order to discuss the wrestling and weight-control programs.

By conditioning one's body to be prepared to wrestle competitively for six or seven minutes, the excess fat a wrestler may have will be lost because of the regular hard work. The fact is that a well-conditioned wrestler, in all probability, is near optimal weight, but not as a result of starving himself or going on a crash diet. He has reduced his body fat by regular training. It is assumed that the wrestler normally eats a well-balanced diet and has appropriate caloric intake. While we are not believers in extreme weight reduction in a short period of time, we do realize the need for a wrestler to lose excess fat, for it is important that a

---

[1]Philip J. Rasch and Walter Kroll, *What Research Tells the Coach about Wrestling* (Washington, D.C.: American Association for Health, Physical Education, and Recreation, 1964).

wrestler arrive at a weight where he will be both physically and mentally efficient in competition.

We would discourage any beginning scholastic wrestler to decide during the summer or off-season at what weight he is going to wrestle. At the high-school level, many boys who wrestle may be involved in football or soccer in the fall. It is our belief that it is good to be involved in athletic activities the entire year. In many other sports, the control of one's weight is not as important as it is in wrestling. Excess fat can even be helpful in some sports. Therefore, a wrestler should not decide at what weight he is going to wrestle until the beginning of the wrestling season (about two months before the first competition) and after he has been given a physical examination by a competent physician.

Professional advice should be given to the wrestler as to the weight class in which he probably will be the most effective. This advice should come as the result of mutual agreement between the team physician and the coach. Contrary to popular belief, the average fat content of high-school and college wrestlers is only about eight percent and seldom more than fifteen percent.[2] Thus, to reduce body fat safely you must have excess fat to lose. A conditioned wrestler will need about five percent body fat for performance and stamina. The team physician, by examining the bone structure, the abdomen, the back of the neck, under the arm, under the chin, and over the eyes, can make a reasonably accurate estimate of the amount of weight a wrestler can safely lose. A simple determination that the wrestler himself can make is to check the skin-fold thickness (by pinching between thumb and forefinger) over his abdomen (horizontal fold about one inch to the right of the umbilicus), the back of his upper arm (vertical fold halfway between shoulder and elbow), and on his forehead (about one inch above his eye). The forehead skinfold thickness serves as the "control" test. All three areas should have about the same thickness of subcutaneous fat. This "pinch test" in the well-conditioned wrestler will usually be about one-half inch for sites other than the forehead, where it is approximately one-quarter inch. If it is much more than one-half inch, it is likely that the athlete has more than eight percent body fat. Of course, final judgement as to the amount of body fat that the athlete has is best determined by a knowledgeable physician.

WEIGHT CONTROL

After a decision has been made about the best weight at which to wrestle, the athlete will want to undertake a program of diet and training. He and his coach must understand that weight control is not a matter of merely crash-reducing for a brief period of time. If reducing is in order, it should take place over a period of several weeks and should be carefully planned. Total weight loss should be at a slow rate—three to four pounds per week is a maximum. Thus, if a wrestler plans on reducing nine pounds, he should expect to achieve this in not less than

---

[2]There is a tendency for the percentage of body fat to increase with the weight class. Thus, a conditioned lightweight wrestler may have as little as five percent body fat, while a conditioned heavyweight wrestler may have as much as ten percent.

three weeks.[3] The majority of scholastic athletes should not lose more than ten percent of their body weight.[4] If fat is lost too rapidly, metabolic acidosis may occur. This is a result of fat being oxidized at too rapid a rate, with ketone bodies forming faster than they can be utilized. The end result is a blood condition that tends to make the wrestler feel below par. Consequently, the athlete will not be in the best condition—either physically or mentally—for competition.

The wrestler's optimum weight should be reached before his first dual meet, and he should stay within a few pounds of this weight throughout the season. Ideally, he should weigh in after a light practice the night before competition at the exact weight (or a little less) for his division. He then will be able to eat a solid nutritious meal that evening of about three pounds (including liquids). These three pounds will be lost by the natural processes of elimination (urine, feces, insensible water loss, etc.) prior to the weigh-in time the next morning or afternoon.

Wrestlers should never plan on taking off the last five or six pounds by dehydration the day before competition. The result of dehydration is the loss of body electrolytes in solution in body fluid which are fundamental for such functions as normal muscle contraction and nerve impulse transmission. Our bodies maintain a balance of the desired concentration of electrolytes by normal excretion. When this normal balance is disturbed through either too rapid or prolonged dehydration, not only is there an unusual loss of electrolytes in the body fluids, but kidney function can be damaged. There can be a loss of blood volume and intracellular-fluid volume with resulting loss of muscular strength and coordination.[5]

For these reasons, it is important that the wrestler plan to make his optimum weight through correction of his caloric intake in concert with a coordinated training program. He should have an understanding of his caloric needs. It is necessary that he maintain an appropriate caloric intake to develop and maintain muscle tone and to provide for body functions. If more calories are ingested than are needed for energy dissipation and growth requirements, they will be stored as fat. Table 6-1 provides a rough guide for the high-school weight classes with regard to the number of calories that should be consumed per day during moderate (but not intense) training in order to maintain the body with its current amount of fat.[6]

A pound of body-fat (adipose tissue) contains about 3500 calories[7] (the same number of calories as in one pound of butter, which, as we know, is primarily

---

[3]Nine pounds may be too much for a given wrestler to lose in three weeks. This figure is provided as a typical example.

[4]Ann Lincoln, *Food for Athletes* (Chicago: Contemporary Books, Inc., 1979).

[5]To assess the effects of rapid weight reduction, Dr. Michael E. Houston studied four university wrestlers who decreased their body weight by eight percent during a four-day period by reducing their food and fluid intake. A significant decrease in muscle glycogen concentration and in dynamic strength was found, but not in aerobid or anaerobic capacity. A three-hour rehydration period did not improve glycogen levels or strength performance.

[6]Adapted from "Maintenance Calorie Chart," in *Eat and Stay Slim* (Meredith Corporation, Better Homes and Gardens Book, 1968), and from Ann Lincoln, *Food for Athletes* (Chicago: Contemporary Books, Inc., 1979).

[7]The term calorie, as used throughout this chapter, is also called great calorie, kilocalorie, and large calorie. It is a quantity of heat equal to 1000 gram-calories.

Table 6–1 Recommended Calorie Intake for Boys 17–19 Years of Age

Weight Class	Daily Maintenance Calorie Intake For Boys 17–19 years	Daily Maintenance Calorie Intake For Boys 14–17 years
98	2300	2700
105	2400	2850
112	2500	3000
119	2650	3200
126	2750	3400
132	2850	3550
138	2950	3700
145	3050	3900
155	3200	4200
167	3400	4500
185	3700	5000
Heavyweight (based on 200–220 lb. wrestler)	4000	5600

animal fat). A carefully planned training program will involve about two hours of rather intense activity per day. The wrestler will "burn up" about 600 calories per hour during his training or approximately 1200 calories per day. The difference between the 1200 calories used in conditioning and daily maintenance calorie intake represents the calories used during the remaining twenty-two hours of the day when normal, routine activities (including sleeping and resting) take place. For example, a 155-pound, 18-year-old wrestler involved in typical work-outs would need about 3200 calories per day if he did not want to lose any of his body fat. However, let us assume he had considerable fat, as confirmed by the team physician, and was certified to wrestle at the 145-pound class. He will want to lose this fat slowly—say, a total weight loss of two and one-half pounds a week for the next four weeks. He will not want to lose these ten pounds by dehydration, but through a moderate caloric deficit program. Since he decided to lose two and one-half pounds per week, his calorie intake per day can easily be computed:

Daily maintenance calorie intake = 3200 calories
Planned weight loss per day = 2.5 pounds/7 days = 0.357 pounds/day
0.357 pounds × 3500 = 1250 calories/per day reduction
Calorie intake per day to lose weight at planned schedule: 3200 − 1250 = 1950 calories/day

By eating planned meals that total approximately 1950 to 2000 calories per day, he should be able to lose ten pounds in four weeks.

A helpful formula for 17- to 19-year-old wrestlers to estimate their calorie intake in order to maintain their well-being at a given weight is: $C = 15.55W + 780$, where C = daily calorie intake need, and W = weight class (in pounds) at which he plans to participate. Thus, in our example above: $C = (15.55)(145) + 780 = 3028$ calories. Once the wrestler gets down to the 145-pound class, he should increase his daily intake from 1950 to approximately 3028 calories in order to maintain his well-being. Note that this agrees closely with the Table 6-1 value of 3050 calories shown for the 145-pound class.[8]

The reader should understand that the above table and formula are only guides. There is a difference in size, shape, body metabolism, and, of course, caloric needs among individuals. Each wrestler should develop his own workout schedule and diet based on the above estimators and then make appropriate modification, if necessary, as he follows his own weight schedule. We would like to caution that no wrestler in training should limit his caloric intake to less than 1200 calories per day on a regular basis. It is suggested that each wrestler maintain his own daily weight progress chart, similar to that shown in Table 6-2.

If he finds he is losing weight more rapidly than scheduled and feels weak and always very hungry, he should increase his daily caloric intake. Conversely, if he is losing weight much slower than planned and if his appetite is not particularly demanding, then he should modify his schedule by reducing his daily caloric intake. It is important to understand that weight is often lost in an erratic fashion, depending upon the patterns of water loss. Thus, one should evaluate his weight loss over several days before making calorie intake adjustments.

It is recommended that excess fat be worked off in the two-month period prior to the beginning of the wrestling season by long-term caloric restriction, well-balanced meals, and regular exercise. Then the young wrestler can report for the first practice trim and ready to go while maintaining a nourishing, body-building diet. We believe, especially in scholastic wrestling where the age of the athletes typically ranges from 14 to 19, that more consideration should be given to building the wrestler *up* to a given weight class than to training *down* to a weight class. It is at this age that energy should be provided for increasing the body weight because of an increase in skeletal and muscle mass during normal growth and maturation. The caloric need to support growth is in addition to that for basal metabolism and energy turnover associated with daily activities, including training.

Table 6–2 Daily Weight Progress Chart

Name: Joseph Smith		Certified Weight Class: 145 lb.		
Date	Before Workout	After Workout	Difference	Pertinent Remarks
Sept. 1	157	154.5	2.5	
2	156	154	2.0	
3	155	153.5	1.5	
4	155	153	2.0	
5	156	153	3.0	Attended Labor Day picnic
6	154.5	152.5	2.0	

[8]This formula is developed by linear regression, using the data provided in Table 6-1.

The young wrestler should not be obliged to go without food for twelve hours before his match in order to make weight. If he finds he is continually having to skip rope or run in a heavy sweatsuit prior to weigh-in time, he can be assured he is in the wrong weight class for his own well-being or has not been watching his weight between competitions.

Finally, we wish to warn again against severe dehydration. When there is either rapid or prolonged dehydration, the electrolyte balance in the body is upset. This can lead to weaknesses that the competitive wrestler must avoid, including loss of muscular strength and coordination, lack of mental alertness, and stress on the cardiovascular system.

Adequate water is needed by competing athletes. This is especially true in tournament competition where endurance is important. One's best performance is achieved when one's body water content remains constant and sweat loss is replaced. If this is not done, the body will become dehydrated and fatigued. We recommend that wrestlers drink one to two glasses of orange or other fruit juice after each match. This will not only replace the water lost in the body, but will provide needed nourishment in preparation for the athlete's next match.

DIET

We now want to consider what foods and how much of them the wrestler should consume in order to maintain an appropriate caloric intake. The wrestler's diet must provide all the essential nutrients, including minerals, proteins, carbohydrates, vitamins, and even some fats, in order to develop and maintain a health, strong body.

Proteins are primarily found in meats and dairy products. They are essential both for the growth and repair of body tissue. Carbohydrates come from cereals, vegetables, fruits, and, to a lesser extent, dairy products. They provide the majority of the energy so important to the athlete.

Fats come primarily from the animal fats we consume in meats and dairy products, including eggs. Some fats are necessary in the diet since they provide for essential nervous and other functions, as well as a reservoir of energy. The wrestler regularly utilizes fatty acids that come from stored fat as he exercises.

Vitamin A is found in fish-liver oils, livers of domesticated animals, and milk. In the vegetable kingdom, their precursors, the carotenes occur. These are converted into vitamin A by the body. Although the carotenes are widely distributed in the vegetable family, the leafy vegetables, including spinach, dandelion, chard, and parsley, are especially good sources. Vitamin A is essential for normal growth and skeletal development, particularly for bone tissue and dentin. It has a prophylactic action against infections, including respiratory infections and other viral diseases.

Vitamin D is found in fish-liver oils, fortified milk, and vegetables. It helps to regulate the calcium and phosphorous balance by direct action on phosphorous metabolism, and it is essential for normal bone and cartilaginous growth.

There are seven known forms of vitamin E that are widely distributed in green plants. Whole grain cereals that contain oats, barley, rye, and wheat germ are especially good sources. Vitamin E is thought to help maintain healthy kidneys, muscle tone, and good respiratory function.

Several naturally occurring forms of vitamin K are found chiefly in the green vegetables, including the cabbage family, spinach, and, to a lesser extent, tomatoes and fruits. Vitamin K is involved in the blood coagulation mechanism and is considered to be necessary in small amounts in a well-balanced diet.

There are nine different compounds in the vitamin B complex. Vitamin B_1 (thiamine) occurs in plants in free form and is available through consumption of yeast, wheat germ, wholemeal wheat or rye bread, soybeans, and pork fat. It is also found in peas, lima beans, and asparagus. Vitamin B_2 (riboflavin) occurs in yeast, liver, milk, fish, and is widely distributed in all leafy vegetables. Particularly good sources of riboflavin are spinach, broccoli, and asparagus. B_3 (niacin) is also found in the vegetable family, including peas, lima beans, and asparagus. We need not discuss the other six members of the vitamin B complex.

The vitamin B family is important for normal body growth and the facilitation of carbohydrate and protein metabolism. These vitamins are also involved in the release of energy, making them especially important to the wrestler.

Vitamin C is widely distributed in nature, especially in both green plants and citrus fruits. Those plants providing particularly large amounts include brussels sprouts, cress, green peppers, broccoli, cauliflower, pears, plums, oranges, grapefruit, and lemons. Vitamin C has a positive effect on normal growth through its influence on the morphology of body tissues. It also provides an anti-infection action by the stimulation of the formation of antibodies. Thus it is thought by some to reduce the severity of colds and offers some protection against other bacterial and viral infections. It also appears to provide an anti-stress factor which allows an individual to adapt more readily to an unusual or strange environment.

Table 6-3 provides a guide as to the recommended daily dietary allowances for young male athletes between 11 and 22 years of age.

We will comment on only two of the many minerals that are involved in a well-balanced diet: iron and potassium. Iron is a vital part of hemoglobin, which carries oxygen to the body cells. Thus, it is important in converting the food we eat into energy. The recommended daily allowance for young male athletes is 10 to 18 mg. Good sources of iron are liver, whole grains, spinach, sundried peas and beans, and lima beans.

Potassium appears to play an important role in eye-hand coordination and thus is essential to the sound functioning of muscles and nerves. It is one of the eletrolytes present in body fluids. Although no recommended adult dietary allowances have been established, recent studies indicate that 0.8–1.3 g. would be sufficient for normal body requirements. Potassium is widely distributed in foods of both plant and animal origin, so those diets that contain ample carbohydrates and proteins will also have sufficient potassium. Bananas are a particularly good source.

If the healthy, young athlete includes selections from each of the primary food groups in a well-balanced diet, he should have no problem in meeting recommended daily dietary requirements. However, if supplementary vitamins and minerals are required, the kind and amount should be recommended by a qualified physician.

Two planned menus that will normally provide all the necessary vitamins, minerals, proteins, and carbohydrates follow.[9] The first menu is planned to pro-

---

[9]Adapted from Ann Lincoln, *Food for Athletes* (Chicago: Contemporary Books, Inc., 1979).

Table 6–3 Food and Nutrition Board, National Academy of Sciences—National Research Council, Recommended Daily Dietary Allowances.[a] Revised 1980. Designed for the maintenance of good nutrition of practically all healthy people in the U.S.A.

	Age	Weight		Height		Protein	Fat-Soluble Vitamins		
							Vitamin A	Vitamin D	Vitamin E
	(years)	(kg)	(lb)	(cm)	(in)	(g)	(µg RE)[b]	(µg)[c]	(mg α-TE)[d]
Males	11–14	45	99	157	62	45	1000	10	8
	15–18	66	145	176	69	56	1000	10	10
	19–22	70	154	177	70	56	1000	7.5	10

	Age	Weight		Height		Protein	Water-Soluble Vitamins						
							Vitamin C	Thiamin	Riboflavin	Niacin	Vitamin B-6	Folacin[e]	Vitamin B-12
	(years)	(kg)	(lb)	(cm)	(in)	(g)	(mg)	(mg)	(mg)	(mg NE)[f]	(mg)	(µg)	(µg)
Males	11–14	45	99	157	62	45	50	1.4	1.6	18	1.8	400	3.0
	15–18	66	145	176	69	56	60	1.4	1.7	18	2.0	400	3.0
	19–22	70	154	177	70	56	60	1.5	1.7	19	2.2	400	3.0

	Age	Weight		Height		Protein	Minerals					
							Calcium	Phosphorus	Magnesium	Iron	Zinc	Iodine
	(years)	(kg)	(lb)	(cm)	(in)	(g)	(mg)	(mg)	(mg)	(mg)	(mg)	(µg)
Males	11–14	45	99	157	62	45	1200	1200	350	18	15	150
	15–18	66	145	176	69	56	1200	1200	400	18	15	150
	19–22	70	154	177	70	56	800	800	350	10	15	150

[a] The allowances are intended to provide for individual variations among most normal persons as they live in the United States under usual environmental stresses. Diets should be based on a variety of common foods in order to provide other nutrients for which human requirements have been less well defined.

[b] Retinol equivalents. 1 retinol equivalent = 1 µg retinol or 6 µg β carotene.

[c] As cholecalciferol. 10 µg cholecalciferol = 400 IU of vitamin D.

[d] α-tocopherol equivalents. 1 mg d-α tocopherol = 1 α-TF.

[e] 1 NE (niacin equivalent) is equal to 1 mg of niacin or 60 mg of dietary tryptophan.

vide about 1500 kcal per day and the second about 2000. These menus can serve as the basis for the selection of a balanced diet for the wrestler who is planning to come down to his ideal weight class.

1500 CALORIE THREE-MEAL MENU FOR ONE DAY

Breakfast
>   1 egg boiled, poached, or scrambled, with 1 slice of bacon
>   1 slice of toast with 1 teaspoon of butter
>   ½ banana or ½ grapefruit or 1 orange
>   1 glass of skim milk

Lunch
>   1 roast beef sandwich involving 3 ounces of beef, 2 slices of bread, and 2 teaspoons of butter, or 3 ounces of ham, liver, pork, veal, turkey, or chicken with 2 slices of

buttered bread

1 tossed salad (greens of all kinds are fine), 1 tablespoon of French or Italian salad dressing

1 glass of skim milk

1 apple *or* ½ banana *or* 12 grapes

Dinner

1 portion involving 4 ounces of fish (cod, halibut, flounder, trout, etc.) *or* beef, chicken, pork, or veal

1 portion (½ cup) of either carrots, peas, squash, onions, turnips, or beets

1 portion of beans (green or wax), broccoli, brussels sprouts, cabbage, etc.

1 slice of bread with butter *or* ½ cup of potatoes (baked or boiled)

1 glass of skim milk

1 dish of gelatin *or* ½ cup of sherbert

2000 CALORIE THREE-MEAL MENU FOR ONE DAY

Breakfast

1 egg boiled, poached, or scrambled, with 2 slices of bacon

1 portion (¾ cup) of dry cereal *or* ½ cup cooked cereal (non-caloric sweetener)

1 slice of toast with 1 teaspoon of butter

½ banana *or* ½ grapefruit *or* 1 orange

1 glass of skim milk

Lunch

1 roast beef sandwich involving 4 ounces of beef, 2 slices of bread, and 2 teaspoons of butter *or* 4 ounces of ham, liver, pork, veal, turkey, or chicken with two slices of buttered bread.

1 tossed salad (greens of all kinds are fine) and 1 tablespoon of French or Italian salad dressing

1 glass of skim milk

1 apple *or* 12 grapes *or* ½ banana

Dinner

1 portion involving 6 ounces of fish (cod, halibut, flounder, trout, etc.) *or* beef, chicken, pork, or veal

1 portion (½ cup) of potatoes (boiled or baked) *or* ¼ cup of corn, baked beans, or lima beans

2 slices of bread with butter

1 portion (½ cup) of either carrots, peas, squash, onions, turnips, or beets

1 portion of beans (green or wax), broccoli, brussels sprouts, cabbage, etc.

1 glass of skim milk

1 portion of sherbert or gelatin

At the end of the wrestling season, it may be desirable to reduce the caloric intake. Unless this is done, there is usually a slow but steady increase in the percentage of body fat and a decrease in the percentage of muscle.

TRAINING PROGRAM

The training program to be undertaken by the successful wrestler has five objectives:

1. To improve muscular strength
2. To improve respiratory capacity and cardiovascular endurance

3. To improve quickness
4. To improve balance and poise
5. To learn thoroughly the principal holds, pinning combinations, and escape methodologies

A training program will vary throughout the year. Initially, the program will be directed toward strength development. Later on, the emphasis will be on developing skills in preparation for dual meets. Late in the season, no new techniques will be undertaken but the emphasis will be on development of stamina in preparation for tournament competition.

Ideally, the wrestler should begin an intensive weight-lifting program about two months before regular competition in order to develop his strength. This would involve weight-lifting for a period of about thirty minutes every other day. On the other days, he should run about five miles in order to develop stamina.[10]

About one month before regular competition begins, the wrestler should change his routine to two-hour workouts daily. Many high-school wrestling programs begin daily practice about a month prior to the first match. These two hours do not have to be consecutive, although normally they would be so that coaching efficiency can be maintained. If, however, there are days a wrestler is unable to be at practice after school in the afternoon, he should plan ahead to have a two-hour workout in the morning prior to going to school or later that same evening. If he is unable to schedule a block of time for two consecutive hours in any given day, he should schedule two workouts per day, each lasting about one hour.

A recommended typical routine is given in Table 6-4.

Perhaps the most important reason for regular, conscientious practice is to get the wrestler in superb condition. This is accomplished primarily by improving the wrestler's lung volume or vital capacity. Regular running and rope-skipping are especially useful in the improvement of vital capacity. We are certain that some of our readers have witnessed many wrestling matches where the more talented contestant lost because of inferior conditioning.

After running and skipping rope (for about 15 minutes), routine conditioning exercises (frequently referred to as warm-up exercises) should be performed for a period of ten to fifteen minutes. These exercises are extremely important for the development of those muscles frequently used in wrestling. Furthermore, an adequate warm-up will raise the body temperature to a point where the body performs more efficiently. Figure 6-1 shows muscles of major importance to the wrestler. It is essential to remember, however, that the wrestler uses almost all his muscles.

The warm-up and weight-lifting program should involve a series of exercises that both utilize and stretch those muscles and joints employed in the sport. The wrestler needs to develop strength and flexibility simultaneously. By referring to Figure 6-1, you will be able to identify the muscles located in the hands, wrists, forearms, shoulders, chest, neck, thighs, calves, and ankles that are most frequently involved.

It is a good idea to alternate "development" exercises (such as push-ups and chin-ups) with exercises that "loosen and stretch" the muscles and joints (such

---

[10] The young wrestler should slowly work up to running this distance. Initially, running five miles may produce excessive fatigue for the scholastic wrestler.

Table 6-4 Recommended Daily Workout Routine

Exercise	Time	Beneficial Results	Conditioning
Run (one mile)	5½ to 6½ min.	Endurance, respiratory fitness, strengthen leg muscles, cardiovascular fitness	Aerobic (requiring the presence of oxygen)
Skip rope	10 min.	Arm-leg coordination, improve balance and timing, promote endurance	Aerobic
Routine conditioning exercises	10 min.	Muscle tone, quickness, agility, improve strength and flexibility	Largely Anaerobic (not requiring the presence of oxygen)
Weight lifting (to be done just one day per week, four days before competition)	10 min.	Improve strength	Largely Anaerobic
Technique drills	30 min.	Quickness, poise, balance, agility, improve strength and flexibility	Largely Anaerobic
Learning new techniques	25 min.	Development and application of new methodologies	Largely Anaerobic
Competitive matches	30 min.	Development of technology, strength, poise, quickness, and endurance	Aerobic and Anaerobic
Conditioning drills	10 min.	Flexibility, quickness, agility, conditioning	Aerobic and Anaerobic

as arm swings, toe-touch, hurdler's stretch, etc.). In Art Keith's book *Complete Book of Wrestling Drills and Conditioning Techniques,* a routine of fifty exercises used in wrestling programs in Japan is well illustrated in sequence photographs. A useful description is provided. Most of these exercises should be performed regularly in connection with the recommended conditioning routine.

Following the warm-up period, approximately thirty minutes should be utilized in connection with technique drills. Here, the wrestler will practice both stance and movements. Time will be spent on both offensive and defensive maneuvers. For example, there will be practice in getting your opponent off balance, throws to the mat from standing, attacking holds from the contact position, and defensive maneuvers from the "being controlled" position.

For a period of fifteen to twenty minutes, the wrestler should be taught new techniques. These are not techniques that are necessarily unknown to the wrestler, but they are those he has not perfected. The coach should not introduce new methods and techniques until the old ones have been thoroughly understood and practiced. When new holds and combinations are introduced, he should demonstrate only a few at any practice session. The key to success is

Figure 6-1 Muscles of Importance in Wrestling

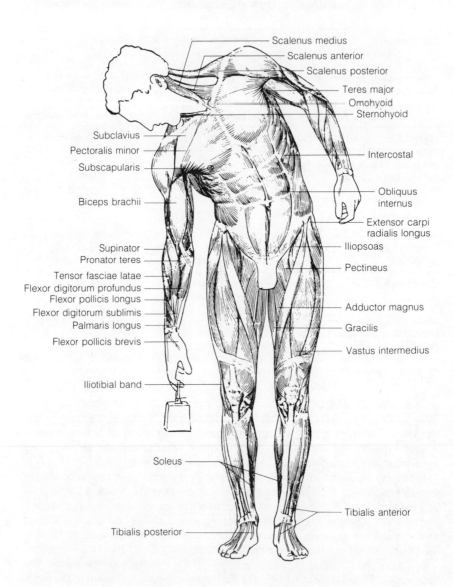

Scalenus medius
Scalenus anterior
Scalenus posterior
Teres major
Omohyoid
Sternohyoid
Subclavius
Pectoralis minor
Subscapularis
Intercostal
Biceps brachii
Obliquus internus
Extensor carpi radialis longus
Supinator
Iliopsoas
Pronator teres
Pectineus
Tensor fasciae latae
Flexor digitorum profundus
Flexor pollicis longus
Flexor digitorum sublimis
Adductor magnus
Palmaris longus
Gracilis
Flexor pollicis brevis
Vastus intermedius
Iliotibial band
Soleus
Tibialis anterior
Tibialis posterior

Figure 6-1 Continued

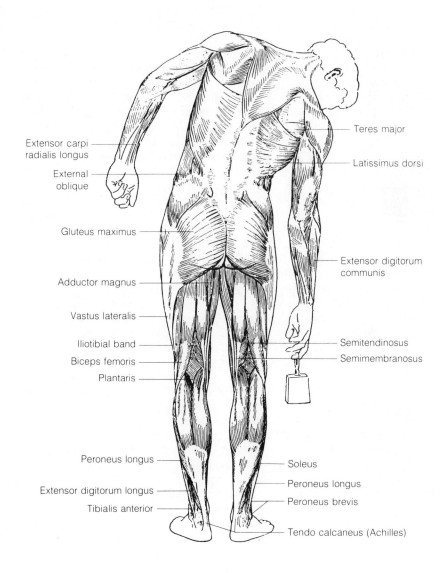

Extensor carpi radialis longus

External oblique

Gluteus maximus

Adductor magnus

Vastus lateralis

Iliotibial band

Biceps femoris

Plantaris

Peroneus longus

Extensor digitorum longus

Tibialis anterior

Teres major

Latissimus dorsi

Extensor digitorum communis

Semitendinosus

Semimembranosus

Soleus

Peroneus longus

Peroneus brevis

Tendo calcaneus (Achilles)

complete mastery of a limited number of techniques rather than a superficial knowledge of a large number.

After working on new techniques, the wrestler should devote the next thirty minutes to intensive wrestling. These practice matches should involve opponents of about the same weight and ability. Such "well-matched" practices will not only more realistically simulate dual-meet competition, but will help prevent injuries sometimes caused by gross mismatches in size and ability.

Wrestling is, to a considerable extent, an anaerobic sport. This means that the body obtains considerable energy during competition from the breakdown of carbohydrates (largely from glycogen stored in the liver and in the muscles themselves) to lactic acid, with a transfer of energy associated with the use of adenosine triphosphate (ATP) and development of heat.[11] The term "anaerobic" means "without oxygen," since this metabolism does not use oxygen in the process. Adequate carbohydrate intake is necessary to replace utilized glycogen.

On the other hand, aerobic "with oxygen" metabolism results in the release of large quantities of energy and the formation of considerable ATP.

The athlete then has three energy systems to utilize. These are adenosine triphosphate degradation to phosphocreatine (ATP-PC), which is anaerobic; the formation of lactic acid from glycogen or glucose which is also anaerobic; the utilization of oxygen, which is aerobic. The body uses all three of these energy transfer mechanisms. However, the proportion changes with the duration of the activity. For example: Camaione and Tillman have estimated that, for six minutes of activity (the length of a scholastic bout), 20 percent of the energy consumed would have its source as ATP-PC, 55 percent from the degradation of glycogen or glucose to lactic acid, and 25 percent from the utilization of oxygen. If the duration of the activity were increased to ten minutes, then 20 percent of the energy would come from the ATP-PC system, 40 percent from the lactic acid system, and 40 percent from oxidation. The training routine suggested earlier has been designed to increase utilization of all three of the energy transfer systems.

Late in the season when preparing for tournament competition, an occasional "day off" is recommended. The familiar phrase "all work and no play can make Johnny a dull boy" certainly applies to wrestling. This personal relaxation tends to provide both physical and mental stimulation. Pre-tournament practices should be brisk and short in relation to running, skipping rope, and routine exercises. These practices should emphasize tournament-type matches.

We cannot emphasize too strongly the importance of the conditioning and training program. Invariably, the championship performer is the conscientious, dedicated athlete who recognizes that most matches are won and lost, not on the day of the match, but in the training program preceding the contest.

[11]David N. Camaione and Kenneth Tillman, *Teaching and Coaching Wrestling: A Scientific Approach*, Second edition (New York: John Wiley and Sons, 1980).

7

Psychological Preparation

The mind is its own place and in itself
can make a heaven of hell, a hell of heaven.
—John Milton,
Paradise Lost

We have learned how a wrestler selects the weight class that suits him best; how he makes his weight; how he trains to develop strength, stamina, flexibility, and quickness; and how he masters the principal holds. We have one point yet to cover before the wrestler is completely ready for competition, and that is the development of mental preparedness. Mental attitude is extremely important in all sports and especially in the sport of wrestling. The power of positive thinking and the setting of goals—not just the goal of winning a match, but training goals such as strength, stamina, and endurance—are very important.

The successful coach, in applying the psychology of coaching, is primarily interested in influencing his athletes in the most desirable fashion. Thus, success as a coach cannot be measured only by trophies and the win/loss record. Often coaches underestimate their influence on young athletes. The coach frequently occupies an important role in the life of his pupils.

THE HUMAN BRAIN

Figure 7-1 illustrates a cross section of the inner brain. The thalamus can be thought of as a sensory relay station. The cerebellum, located near the back of the head, controls muscle movements. At the head of the brain stem are the pons and the midbrain, which govern both sleep and wakefulness; and below them is the medulla, which regulates breathing and heart action. The part of the brain that we will be most interested in is the amygdala, which is generally thought to be the center that controls aggression or docility.

Figure 7-2 illustrates the outer brain, which is composed of four parts or lobes: frontal lobe, temporal lobe, parietal lobe, and occipital lobe. All four lobes combined are called the cerebral cortex, considered to be the seat of consciousness. Since the frontal lobe controls all voluntary movement, we are particularly concerned with its activity. This lobe also controls the sense of smell and the mechanics of speech. The temporal lobe governs hearing, language comprehen-

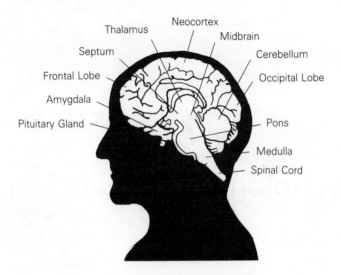

Figure 7-1   The Inner Brain

sion, and certain types of memory. The parietal lobe is concerned with the sense of touch and body perception, while the occipital lobe regulates vision.

The whole brain is composed of two halves called the cerebral hemispheres. These hemispheres are connected by a thick bundle of two hundred million nerve fibers which are called the corpus callosum. The right cerebral hemisphere controls the left side of the body, and the left cerebral hemisphere controls the right side. The left hemisphere is usually the dominant portion, since it is the center of logic and speaking ability.

Only a nervous system as elaborate as man's allows the skilled performance of wrestling, with its constant demand of both physical and mental activity. One can only marvel when he considers what a finely tuned instrument the human body is. This mechanism involving hydraulic, pneumatic, mechanical, and electrical systems, all closely integrated by relaying intelligence through the brain, simultaneously regulates the heartbeat, respiration, body metabolism, aggressive moves, counters, deploys—all performed in fractions of a second, and each involving different but controlled sets of muscles.

AVOIDING ANXIETY

When confronted by such a complex decision-making and control system as the human brain, with its more than ten billion nerve cells, one may have some qualms about how best to provide advice to the athlete so that he is adequately prepared mentally for dual-meet and tournament competition. In the past, a rousing pep talk from the coach was all that took place, and often this was all that was needed by many of the participants to perform at their best level of capability. Today, we ask how one really gets "psyched up" so that he performs, not at his peak, but better than his supposed peak performance. We have all heard stories of mediocre athletes who, in some way, gained the mental prepared-

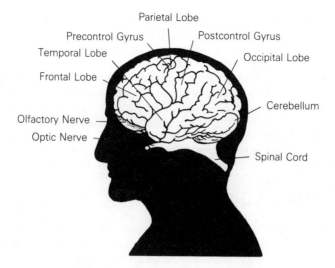

Figure 7-2 The Outer Brain (lateral view)

ness to exceed their normal capabilities. What every coach would like is to get his team in a mental frame of mind so that this "better than probable" level of performance will be forthcoming.

Many people do not really have a feeling for the tremendous pressure put on athletes today. This pressure comes from the coaches, the athlete's peers, the fans, and the athlete's family. When this pressure builds up to a certain level, it becomes counter-productive to the athlete. He begins to believe that he is not capable of performing as expected and "as required" according to his coach. We all have read about athletes who have resorted to using amphetamines as a psychological lift to restore confidence. The problem is that too much tension has been put on the athlete. He doesn't need more tension—he needs more confidence. This is especially true if he suffered a humiliating defeat in his last match. Interaction with coaches and parents can be a major source of stress and anxiety for the wrestler. Coaches and parents, in their relationships with athletes, should endeavor to create a positive interpersonal environment, thus minimizing the generation of stress.

BUILDING CONFIDENCE

We believe that a wrestler should enter each contest confident that he will perform up to the level of his full potential. The coaching staff and his parents have an obligation to provide guidance to help the wrestler be in tune with himself, have emotional composure and self-confidence. In order to provide the right stimulation—to ask the right questions—it is important that the coach know his athletes.

The same approach to building confidence and eliminating or reducing worries cannot be used with each member of the wrestling squad. The coach should learn which athletes are lacking in self-confidence, which have high outside pressures, which have worries, which have peculiar problems. Instead of a "rah-rah, go get 'em" type of pep talk, perhaps a particular wrestler needs a half hour in solitude followed by a short, refreshing confirmation of his enormous potential. What the wrestler needs is conscious nerve activity through the amygdala (the center of the brain that controls either aggression or docility) with an automatic aggressive response. The right message in one's consciousness can profoundly affect the automatic system of either (1) aggression, with physical follow-through (fight), or (2) docility, with a corresponding lack of physical follow-through (flight). These "fight or flight" reactions, as psychologists refer to them, occur in different degrees depending upon the message interpretation through the brain.

REDUCING STRESS

What is to be avoided is the pep talk that breeds anxiety. If, just prior to a contest, a wrestler who is lacking in self-confidence is told that he "must win," the result is an emotional conflict which induces a state of anxiety or stress. The more severe the emotional conflict (that is, the conflict of "I must win" vs. "I can't beat this guy"), the greater the anxiety. This anxiety produces the symptoms of an accelerated heartbeat, difficulty in breathing, and general fatigue—a condition the athlete cannot afford to be in prior to a match. The result will be a humiliating loss. Before each match, both the wrestler and his coach should reduce the number of stress factors facing the athlete.

It is well known that good sports psychology can teach an athlete to have control over stress and to react properly to it. A successful wrestling coach will help his pupils to establish goals and cope with stress. Thus, to assure that each member of his starting team is psychologically prepared for competition, the coach should spend a few minutes with each athlete individually. The session should be directed toward building the wrestler's confidence, dispelling any worries about the opposition, and getting him to think positively.

The coach must always recognize that the amount of talent a good athlete has is an intangible. His range of performance is considerable. On a given day, he may be capable of beating any of the top ten wrestlers in the country; and on a different day, he is equally capable of losing to an athlete who, on the average, is not nearly as skilled or proficient. For example, wrestler C is a much better performer than A most of the time and better than B a good share of the time. Yet, it is possible for A to out-perform C some of the time and to beat B a significant portion of the time.

When a wrestler is facing an opponent who has a much better record than his own, he should understand that his opponent also is capable of wrestling at an inferior level. The coach will want to assure his wrestler that his potential may be much better than he thinks. He will want to point out that the wrestler has the necessary conditioning, skill, and desire to win, and, if he will give maximum effort, he may very well emerge the victor.

AFTER A LOSS

If the wrestler loses, it is important that his coach accept the loss in a manner that will not be detrimental to the future performance of his pupil. He must recognize that the loss will decrease the confidence of his wrestler, and a restoration of confidence is absolutely essential to put a slumping athlete back on the winning track. The coach should endeavor to develop in his wrestlers a positive desire to achieve, rather than to fear failure.

Immediately after the losing wrestler returns to the bench, his coach should shake his hand and offer some words of encouragement. He should refrain from making any remarks that would lead the wrestler to believe that it is necessary to win-at-any-cost. The next day the coach should talk quietly to his defeated

Table 7–1 Response Categories Of Coaching Behavior

	1	Response To Desirable Performance
	a	Reinforcement—a positive rewarding action to a good effort or move
	b	Nonreinforcement—failure to respond to a good performance
REACTIVE BEHAVIORS	2	Response to Mistakes
	a	Mistake—contingent encouragement—encouragement given to a wrestler following a defeat or a mistake
	b	Mistake—contingent technical instruction—instructing and/or demonstrating to a wrestler how to correct a move or a mistake he has made
	c	Punishment—a negative reaction, verbal or nonverbal, following poor performance or a mistake
	d	Punitive technical instruction—technical instruction following a mistake which is given in a punitive manner
	e	Ignoring mistakes—failure to respond to a player mistake, loss, or demonstration of poor performance
	3	Response to Misbehavior
	a	Keeping control—reactions intended to restore or maintain order among team members
	4	Match-related
	a	General technical instruction—spontaneous instruction in the techniques and strategies (not following a mistake)
SPONTANEOUS BEHAVIORS	b	General encouragement—spontaneous encouragement (not following a mistake)
	c	Organization—administration behavior which sets the stage for strategies for up-coming matches
	5	Match-irrelevent
	a	General communication—interactions with wrestlers and other personnel unrelated to the match taking place at the moment

Adapted from Frank L. Smoll and Ronald E. Smith, "Psychologically-Oriented Coach Training Programs: Design, Implementation, and Assessment," *Annual Publication of the North American Society for the Psychology of Sport and Physical Activity,* 1979.

performer, pointing out both the strong and weak areas of performance and how the match was lost. He should emphasize that his wrestler has the potential to win and, if he gets to meet the same adversary again, his probability of winning will be much higher. He should explain that this loss can even be profitable. Often a tough loss is a better learning experience than an easy win.

We have mentioned the desirability of having the coach spend some time privately with each member of the team immediately before and immediately after each contest. It is also desirable to address the team as a whole just prior to a match and again the day following the contest. These meetings, too, should be planned to build confidence and relax tensions. It should be pointed out that the team as a whole is skilled, well-trained, and in excellent condition, that the staff only expects each participant to do his best, that with their best performance winning is as sure to come as night follows day. It should also be emphasized that winning is not the main objective, but rather giving one's best performance. If this objective is realized, then the wrestler, his coaching staff, and his parents should be rightfully proud.

CONCLUSION

Research has proven that there are specific relationships between coaching behaviors and athlete's reactions to their contest experience.[1] The successful coach will use psychology in order to completely develop his players. His major aim should be to have his wrestlers give their maximum effort in striving to win. Thus his goal is to obtain this effort, not to stress winning itself.

Experience has shown that positive approaches are usually more effective than punitive behaviors and non-enforcement for obtaining maximum effort. The positive approach will emphasize the use of reinforcement for effort as well as performance, the giving of encouragement after mistakes, and the provision of technical instruction in an encouraging fashion (see Table 7-1).

Usually, punishment—whether it be a negative reaction, verbal or nonverbal—following a mistake will not be nearly as effective as instructing or demonstrating to a wrestler how to correct a mistake he has made.

---

[1]Frank L. Smoll and Ronald E. Smith, "Psychologically—Oriented Coach Training Programs: Design, Implementation, and Assessment," *Annual Publication of the North American Society for the Psychology of Sport and Physical Activity,* 1979.

8

Officiating the Match

Four things belong to a judge: to hear courteously, to answer wisely, to consider soberly, and to decide impartially.

—Socrates

In the sport of wrestling, the one official is under close scrutiny by an audience that is physically rather close to his arena of operation. The entire wrestling match is conducted within a field of vision comprising a circle only six to eight feet in diameter, also one that remains relatively stable in location. (Compare other sports; even fencing and boxing involve more spatial movement.) Thus, each spectator can concentrate on every detail of the match, make his own evaluations of the progress of the bout, and compare his own interpretations of rules and regulations to those of the official.

In most other "spectator" sports, there are two or more officials, the field of activity is much larger, and the focus of attention is constantly changing. In addition, spectators are usually farther from the center of activity and therefore the officials are not under the same pressure as when the audience is literally "on the referee's back." The closer the spectators are to the official, the greater the intensity of challenges to the official's interpretations of the rules.

NATURE OF WRESTLING RULES

The nature of the rules in wrestling necessitate many judgment evaluations. A strike in baseball occurs when the ball crosses home plate somewhere between the knees and the armpits of the batter. This "strike zone" is not only easily understood by the spectators, but its interpretation is reasonably objective. Compare the calling of a ball or strike by the umpire with the calling of a penalty point by the referee because the wrestler in the advantage position on the mat has not made an honest attempt to secure a fall in the past twenty seconds. As you have learned reading Chapter 3, many of the rules and regulations in both high-school and collegiate wrestling require subjective interpretation by the official. What is stalling to one official may not be to another. What is a potentially dangerous hold to one referee may not be to another. What is a near-fall to one referee is not necessarily a near-fall to another, and so on. Even the top coaches in the country would not be in perfect agreement as to the interpretation of all the rules and regulations or even as to what constitutes superior wrestling ability.

From the above discussion, you can readily see that the referee in wrestling has an arduous task for three reasons:

1. The ability of the fans to witness clearly what is happening during the entire match.
2. The close proximity of the fans to the field of action.
3. The fact that judgement must constantly be exercised in the interpretation of many of the rules.

REQUIREMENTS FOR BEING A GOOD REFEREE

One might ask, then, what are the major requirements that a good referee must meet to handle all of this? There are four major requirements. First and foremost, he should thoroughly know the existing rules. Since rules are continually changing and new ones are regularly being added, the competent referee has a formidable task. It is extremely important that every official maintain contact with the National Federation of State High School Association Rules Advisory Committee and the NCAA Rules Committee so that he will always be cognizant of any addition, deletion, or change in the rules.

It is one thing to know the rules, but it is something else to know wrestling. The second requirement for being a good official is that he should know wrestling from personal experience in order to apply the rules effectively. His experience as a wrestler need not have been at championship level, but it must have been either at the high-school or collegiate level and for long enough so that he has more than a superficial knowledge of the sport. The more experience the official has had as a wrestler, the better he will "know" the sport. The officials that we believe do an exceptionally good job have all had between eight and twelve years of experience as wrestlers. In our opinion, it would seem that the minimum experience that an official should have as a wrestler is two years.

The third characteristic of the sound wrestling referee is accuracy. His interpretation of the rules should be correct, not just a high proportion of the time, but virtually all the time. Accuracy seems to be a characteristic of the knowledgeable, experienced referee. In order to get the experience to become accurate, the neophyte official should contact a local high school or college and work with the team by helping to officiate nightly scrimmage and elimination bouts. The local coaching staff will welcome his support, and the "green" official will be obtaining essential experience. Also, there is often an officials' association in the area, where training programs are offered to new officials to help them to gain accuracy.

The fourth and final characteristic of the good referee is consistency. As mentioned previously, different officials will interpret some of the rules differently. Those rules that apply to situations at the edge of the mat are the most controversial. For example, the present out-of-bounds rule states: "When a supporting part of both wrestlers is out-of-bounds, wrestling shall be stopped and wrestlers returned to the center of the mat and started according to the position of each at the time they went out-of-bounds." There will not necessarily be consistency on this rule, since the identification of a supporting part of the body will differ among the officials. Further, the rule changes somewhat regarding a pinning situation. However, a given official should be consistent in his interpretation of this and all other rules.

In order for an official to be consistent in his interpretations, he must not be biased in any way. He should guard against having any pre-conceived opinions as to which wrestlers are the best and should win. Often an outstanding wrestler with an unblemished record will carry what we refer to as the "halo effect." The wrestler is known to be good, and is expected to win. It is very easy, in such a case, for an inexperienced official to make judgement calls to the advantage of the favorite. "After all, isn't he the better wrestler?" the inexperienced official will rationalize.

PERSONAL CHARACTERISTICS

In addition to the above four characteristics of knowing the rules, knowing wrestling, accuracy, and consistency, the successful official needs to have certain personal characteristics, both in appearance and behavior.

The official should have a clean, neat physical appearance. He should wear a clean, pressed, official uniform and a good pair of wrestling shoes. His physical appearance will then command respect from all those in attendance. This also means that he should be in reasonably good condition and not excessively overweight. Officiating is an energy-consuming activity, and the official must be in proper condition to handle the rigors of the responsibility. Related to the matter of appearance is the equipment the official should carry. Although a small point, this, too, helps establish his professionalism. Instead of reaching in his pocket for a coin, he will make a better impression if he flips a decision disc expressly designed for this purpose. It is also a good idea to carry a spare whistle. Occasionally, a whistle will fail to work, and they are easily misplaced or even lost. Nothing can get a referee off to a poorer start than having to look for his whistle at the beginning of the match.

OFFICIATING THE MATCH

During the course of officiating a match, the referee should make all of his announcements clearly and emphatically. Simultaneously, he should confirm his announcement with the appropriate visual signal (see Figure 8-1). It is very important that he not anticipate what he thinks is going to happen and thus make an erroneous call. Occasionally, an official awards a "take down" prior to either wrestler actually gaining control; or perhaps the offensive wrestler never gets control and the referee responds by awarding an escape which really didn't happen. So, he compounds his error by endeavoring to compensate for it. The experienced referee, upon realizing that he has awarded a takedown prematurely and in error, will stop the match, correct his call, and have both wrestlers continue the match in a neutral position.

The referee, once he has made a call or a decision, should not change it

NATIONAL FEDERATION
WRESTLING OFFICIALS SIGNALS

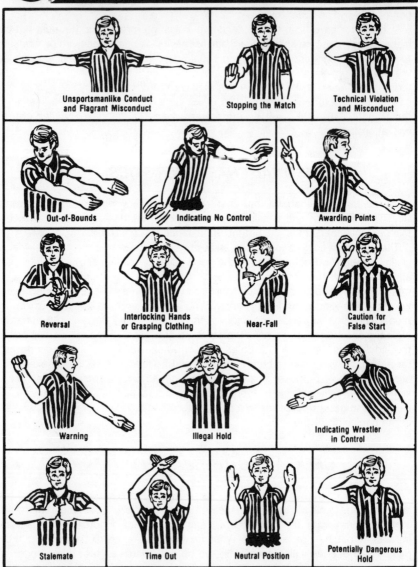

Figure 8-1   Officials' Signals

unless it can be indisputably proved that a mistake was made. For example, he may award a takedown after time has run out. If the timer substantiates that the call was made just after the match was officially over, the referee should reverse his call (see Table 8-1).

Table 8–1 Wrestling Scorers and Timers Instructions*

The official scorer shall be seated at the officials' table and be responsible for: (a) recording points scored by each contestant when signalled by the referee; (b) recording the choice of the wrestler in the advantage position at the start of the second and third periods; (c) constantly checking the visiting teams' scorer; (d) immediately advising the match time-keeper when there is any disagreement regarding the score; (e) advising the scoreboard operator or assistant scorers of the correct score during each match; and (f) presenting the referee with the scorebook at the end of each match.

The assistant scorers are responsible for recording points earned by each individual wrestler during the course of the match. As points are earned in a dual meet, a running team score shall be kept following each individual match.

The match timekeeper is responsible for: (a) keeping the overall time of the match; (b) recording the accumulated time-outs for injury and/or coach-official conferences for review-ing possible misapplication of the rules; (c) notifying the referee after a significant situation has passed and the match is stopped, or for disagreement by official scorer and time-keeper, or when requested by a coach, to discuss a possible error; (d) assisting, when requested by the referee, in determining whether a situation occurred before or after the termination of a period; and (e) when a visual clock is not available, calling the minutes to referee, contestants, and spectators and indicating the number of seconds remaining in the last minute of the period at 15-second intervals.

SCORING ABBREVIATIONS

T_2—Takedown
R_2—Reversal
E_1—Escape
N_2—Near-fall (stopped)
N_3—Near-fall (5 seconds)
P—Penalty
C—Caution
W—Warning
UCT—Unsportsmanlike conduct

FMD—Flagrant misconduct DQ
$\updownarrow$—Position
F—1:38-Fall
For.—Forfeit
Def.—Default
DQ—Disqualified
SD—Superior decision
MD—Major decision
Dec.—Decision
DR—Draw

PENALTY CHART

Infractions	Warning	First Penalty	Second Penalty	Third Penalty	Fourth Penalty	Rule
Illegal Holds	No	1 Pt.	1 Pt.	2 Pts.	Disqualify	7–1
Technical Violations	No	1 Pt.	1 Pt.	2 Pts.	Disqualify	7–3
Stalling	Yes	1 Pt.	1 Pt.	2 Pts.	Disqualify	7–6
Misconduct of Contestants	No	1 Pt.	1 Pt.	2 Pts.	Disqualify	7–4

Table 8–1 *Continued*

Unsportsmanlike Conduct	No	Deduct 1 Team Point	Remove from Premises	(Removal is for duration of dual meet or tournament session only)	8–3
Flagrant Misconduct	No	Disqualify on first offense and deduct 1 team point		Contestant is eliminated from further competition in tournament	8–1–4
Greasy Substance on Skin, Objectionable Pads and Braces, Illegal Equipment or Costume		Disqualify if not removed or corrected in allotted time (3 min.)			3–1–3, 4

SUMMARY OF TECHNICAL VIOLATIONS

Misconduct of Contestants (7–4)

Delaying Match (7–6)

Assuming Incorrect Starting Position (7–3–2)

Going Off Wrestling Area (7–3–3)

Grasping Clothing, Etc. (7–3–4)

Interlocking Hands (7–3–5)

Leaving Mat Without Permission (7–3–7)

NOTE 1. Disqualification due to technical violation, illegal hold, stalling, or misconduct of contestants does not eliminate a contestant from further competition in tournaments. Disqualification for unsportsmanlike conduct eliminates a contestant from the tournament session only. Disqualification for flagrant misconduct eliminates a contestant from further competition in the tournament.

NOTE 2. Points for unnecessary roughness, grasping clothing, or locking hands are awarded in addition to points earned.

EXAMPLE OF INFRACTIONS. Wrestler 'a' in the first period locks hands—penalty, 1 point. Second period, he uses illegal hold—penalty, 1 point. Later in second period he is warned for stalling. In third period, he is called for stalling again—penalty, 2 points. Later in the third period he locks his hands—penalty, disqualification.

*Courtesy of National Federation of State High School Associations

Throughout the contest, the referee should maintain a friendly but firm attitude with both contestants. Likewise, he should not let the spectators rattle him. On occasion, officials over-react to the crowd and award points that have not been earned. The competent official is oblivious to the audience. He never antagonizes the spectators nor does he allow them to influence his calls.

One of the keys to good officiating is to always be in a position to see every detail of each maneuver made by both contestants. This means that the referee will need to move quickly around the mat as the wrestlers change position. It also means that he should be able to anticipate where he should be moving in order to be in the proper position as a sequence of moves is developing.

Certainly, refereeing both scholastic and intercollegiate wrestling is an arduous task. Good officiating is appreciated too infrequently by the fans, coaches, and wrestlers. Yet, good refereeing is essential if the sport is to continue to grow. The majority of refereeing is excellent. The wrestling referee makes a significant contribution, not only to the sport of wrestling, but to the development of fairness, poise, and tolerance in young men.

9

How to Enjoy Wrestling as a Spectator

The real character of a man is found out by his amusements.
—Sir Joshua Reynolds

Men are four:
He who knows not and knows not
he knows not, he is a fool—shun him;
He who knows not and knows he knows not,
he is simple—teach him;
He who knows and knows not he knows,
he is asleep—wake him;
He who knows and knows he knows,
he is wise—follow him!
—Arabic Apothegm

The principal reason we attend any sporting event is to be entertained or amused. Of course, there are other reasons—to see a son, daughter, or friend participate; to show loyalty to a school or institution; and so on. But certainly in the majority of cases, we are in attendance for relaxation, a change of pace, amusement, and entertainment. In order to receive maximum entertainment, we must have an understanding of what is taking place. The more complete that understanding, the more appreciative that spectator will be of superlative performance in the sport being witnessed. For example, one cannot appreciate how difficult it is to do a one-arm chin-up unless he has an understanding of the strength required to perform this feat, and this understanding comes from having tried to do it.

RULES FOR ENJOYING AN ATHLETIC EVENT

The first rule for really enjoying the contest is to have a complete understanding of the sport. This means you should know how the scoring takes place, how the rules and regulations apply, and the principal attributes of the successful performer. Up to this point, you should have learned enough by reading and studying this text to have a good understanding of both collegiate and high-school wrestling. You have learned about the rules and regulations, the officiating, the principal wrestling holds (including the illegal ones), and the training and weight-control program that the wrestler should adopt.

The second requirement for enjoying a wrestling match is to have company. You should take one or more other fans with you or sit with some friend, colleague, or associate. Companionship usually breeds contentment; however, when attending wrestling meets, companionship breeds enjoyment. The fan or fans you sit with should also be at least reasonably knowledgeable of the sport. Sitting with an unknowledgeable fan can be worse than attending the match alone.

The third requirement is to be informed about the strengths and weaknesses of each member of the opposing teams. This, of course, must be done prior to attending the meet. Obtaining this information is relatively easy since almost all of it appears on the sports pages of a good local newspaper. It is a good idea to prepare this information in outline form and bring the summary to the contest with you. The following format is representative of the amount of detail that it is desirable to obtain:

WEIGHT CLASS	HOME TEAM	W	L	D	REMARKS	VISITING TEAM	W	L	D	REMARKS
98	SMITH	5	6	1	Strong but inexperienced	COLE	6	3	0	Has beaten Riddle from Enola
105	JONES	3	8	0	Easily taken down	BARGER	4	6	0	Lost last 2 matches
112	BROWN	11	0	1	Has good single leg	CORBETT	7	4	1	Is a pinner w/ bear hug
119	REED	8	3	0	Good legs	ZEIS	6	5	1	Won last 3 incl. Snow

The more familiar you become with your "home" team, the better fan you will be and the greater your enjoyment while attending both the dual meets and the tournaments.

It is an excellent idea to attend team practices occasionally, if your work schedule permits. This will give you an opportunity to become better acquainted with the coaches, as well as with the individual athletes. As those relationships develop, you will find your enthusiasm and loyalty to "your team" increasing dramatically. A word of caution here: while we advocate attending practice, we do not think you should become so personally involved that you find you are, in effect, competing with the coaches. It is most unlikely that you will become so knowledgeable that you will be able to do a better job than the coach. All coaches welcome your attendance, interest, and participation; but they will not tolerate your interference with a well-designed and carefully conceived program.

The fourth factor for maximizing your enjoyment as a spectator is to develop enthusiasm for the sport and for your team. It is very easy to become enthusiastic for an undefeated team, but how does one develop enthusiasm for a team with a zero and ten or even a four and six record? Perhaps the best way to become enthusiastic is to become involved with the local high-school or university team that you are supporting. Often there is a "Boosters' Club" with which you can become affiliated. This organization meets regularly and reviews the progress of the team's wrestlers individually; films of the most recent match are shown and discussed; and the coming meet or tournament is discussed with consideration of probable wins and losses at the various weight classes. Of course, the head coach and his assistants will be in attendance and will be able to answer questions and provide much information as to the potential of the team. These scheduled meetings often may be a luncheon or dinner meeting and can do much, not only to increase your enthusiasm, but to provide beneficial effects for the young athletes, the coaching staff, and the school.

If you are currently a spectator and no such club has been organized, we suggest you take the initiative and start a Wrestling Booster Club. A core group of fifteen to twenty members is all that is needed. Parents and relatives of the wrestlers are usually eager to join in such a venture. The club must be well organized if it is going to be a viable, productive organization. Its principal objective is to promote the welfare of scholastic and collegiate wrestling, with particular emphasis on the local team. Modest membership dues should be required so they accumulate until something positive can be done for the team. For example, many high schools have not been able to afford films of their meets. The club can purchase a camera and projector and finance the cost of the film. Several of the club members can be responsible for taking the pictures and showing them at the next regular meeting.

BECOMING A GOOD FAN

One of the major benefits of having a Booster Club is to help educate the fans. Too many fans today expect too much from young athletes. They fail to recognize that they are not professionals but are only talented young men who are participating in an *extra*-curricular activity.

Again, too often the irate fan blames the coach and his staff for any lack of success the team may encounter. Such fans seem to be unable to accept the fact that all high-school and college athletes do make mistakes. Fans must be taught that school-boy athletes often make mistakes and never will be perfect. It is because of these mistakes that high-school and collegiate wrestling is both exciting and unpredictable.

Another point that the club will want to emphasize is that, in the majority of cases, especially at the high-school level, the coach is also an educator. He has been taught and trained to be a good teacher—to impart knowledge in his areas of speciality to all students entering his classroom. The fact that he is a coach, too, indicates not only his breadth of competence but his sincere interest in the complete development of young men—intellectual, physical, social, and even spiritual. Too many fans do not take this into account. The really good coach is one who is able to completely develop his students—to bring out the very best in them. The coach, more than anyone else in the gymnasium, wants to win. But he never wants to win at the expense of moral behavior and ethics.

As has already been pointed out, rules and regulations change almost every year. A good fan will keep up-to-date on the rules. He will acknowledge that officials are interpreting rules based upon the latest revisions, additions, and deletions.

Finally, the club will want to teach its members and all fans they come in contact with that they are guests of the institution whose team they are supporting. As such, they should feel privileged to be able to watch the more talented students of two schools exhibit what they have learned in the athletic classroom. The well-educated, considerate fan will learn the rules of the sport, have respect for the officials who have spent an enormous amount of time and effort in preparation, and applaud the talented and courageous athlete no matter which team he represents.

KEEPING SCORE

The last point that we recommend be followed in order to maximize enjoyment as a spectator is to keep a running score of each match. If you use a foremat similar to the Scoring Analysis Summary shown, you will find you can keep this running record during the course of the match and easily follow every motion of both wrestlers. In fact, the adoption of this procedure will cause you to be a more acute observer of the entire contest.

You will find there are several beneficial results of this detailed scorekeeping. First, you will have accumulated substantiating data about how every wrestler won, lost, or tied his match. You will have much more information than merely the winner and the score. This added information is satisfying and will prove to be extremely helpful when discussing details of the match with friends, parents, and the wrestlers themselves. Second, you will find that this progressive scoring will soon make you a more astute fan. You will gain greater appreciation for those special skills that are demonstrated by the quality athlete. Lastly, you will find that, as a spectator, the wrestling matches you attend are more enjoyable. You will develop a feeling both of being entertained and of having made a positive accomplishment.

Note how the Scoring Analysis Summary is used during the contest: In the 98-pound weight class, we have posted the names of the two contestants, Smith and Jones. Columns during each period have been assigned for takedown

WRESTLING SCORING ANALYSIS SUMMARY

WEIGHT CLASS	CONTESTANTS	FIRST PERIOD						SECOND PERIOD						THIRD PERIOD						OVERTIME					
		T	E	R	P	F	S	T	E	R	P	F	S	T	E	R	P	F	S	T	E	R	P	F	S
98	DOUG SMITH	✓					2						2	✓✓					7						
	ED JONES	✓					1	✓✓					5						5						
105																									
112																									
119																									

(T), escape (E), reversal (R), predicament (P), penalty point (F), and score at the end of that period (S). As soon as Doug Smith scored a takedown, a small check was made by the spectator in the T column. When Ed Jones escaped later in that same period, a check was made under the E column. This was all the scoring that occurred in the first period, and Smith led 2 to 1. If a second takedown had been made by Smith in this period, a second check under the column T would have been made. It is apparent in reviewing the record that Smith won the match 7–5. He scored a takedown in the first period, nothing in the second period, and a reversal and a three-point predicament in the final period. His opponent, Ed Jones, had an escape in the first period, a reversal and a two-point predicament in the second period, and no scoring in the third period to garner a total of five points—not enough to win. It should be obvious how meaningful this type of record of each match can be.

10

Great Wrestlers of the Modern Era

Unbounded courage and compassion
join'd,
Tempering each other in the victor's
mind,
Alternately proclaim him good and
great,
And make the hero and the man
complete.
—Joesph Addison
(1672–1719), "The Campaign"

In all sports, the caliber of the participants seems to improve dramatically with every passing decade. As great as Jack Dempsey and Joe Louis were, it is questionable how many rounds either could have survived against Mohammad Ali when he was at his peak. There is little question in the authors' minds that big Bill Tilden would be unable to win a set from the likes of Borg, Connors, or McEnroe. Most world track-and-field records are shattered within a decade. Red Grange would probably not be able to compete with the likes of Jim Brown, who still holds the all-time rushing record in professional football. In all probability, Jim Brown's great performance will in time be overshadowed by someone like Walter Payton, Earl Campbell, or another promising young running back. Wrestling is no exception. The poise, agility, speed, and technique of today's wrestlers on the average exceed what was characteristic just a decade ago. Of course, occasionally a really great athlete appears on the scene who will outperform contenders for a decade or more—for example, Jesse Owens's 60-yard-dash record was not broken for forty years.

Just how far back should we go to tell a little about the really good amateur wrestlers of the modern era? It was originally our intention to identify several of the stellar wrestlers of the past twenty years. However, there is a feeling of nostalgia as we relate the exploits of such Oklahoma State greats as Uetake, Roderick, Henson, Hutton, Peery, Flood, VanBebber, Collins, Keen, and Lookabaugh. Of these, Stanley Henson, three-time NCAA champion (1937, 1938, 1939), might be considered by many old-time fans as the greatest American wrestler in this century. Then, too, those U.S. Olympic champions who distinguished themselves, in early days—for instance, Douglas Blubaugh, Terence McCann, and Shelby Wilson in 1960, or William Smith in 1952, or Henry Wittenberg and Glen Brand in 1948—should perhaps be discussed at this time. Other greats that come to mind include Dan Hodge of the University of Oklahoma, Bill Koll of Iowa State Teachers College, Peter Blair of Navy, Frank Bettucci of Cornell, Eddie Eichelberger of Lehigh, just to name a few.

As good as these early wrestlers were, it is our feeling that we can confine our reminiscing to a few of the top wrestlers of the past dozen years or so. The following names stand out as the real "class" wrestlers of this era: Stan Dziedzic, Dan Gable, Lee Kemp, Mark Lieberman, Ben Peterson, John Peterson, Rick Sanders, Wade Schalles, Gray Simons, and Wayne Wells. We are certain that several other names should be included, but certainly this sample of ten is representative of the best wrestling talent of the modern era.

Following is a short history of the wrestling performance of each of these wrestling greats. Included are their personal comments, which will provide some insight into their lifestyles, mental discipline, and philosophies that contributed to their remarkable performances.

STAN DZIEDZIC

Stan Dziedzic, national coach of the AAU/USA wrestling team and the 1977 World Free-style Champion at 163 pounds, was named Amateur Wrestling's "Man of the Year" for 1979 during the 1980 NCAA Division I wrestling championships at Oregon State University.

Like most great competitors, Stan began wrestling at an early age (14), while a junior-high-school student. In senior high school, where he wrestled at the 120, 127, and 133-pound weight classes, he began to develop the tenacity and desire that is so important in this sport. Although he was never a state champion, it was apparent that he would develop into a great wrestler. He demonstrated the enthusiasm, mental toughness, and will to win that always is evident in the really great wrestlers.

While wrestling for Slippery Rock State College (Pennsylvania), he won three NCAA College Division championships and one Division I title en route to a 118–2 win-loss record. He was a bronze medalist in the Olympics and is a two-time World Cup winner (1975 and 1977) and World Games winner (1977). Stan's most effective strategy is the single-leg takedown, which he blends with a rhythmic sequence that begins as a defensive counter.

What advice does Stan Dziedzic offer to young men who aspire to the role of champion? Stan told the authors that dedication to the sport is essential. One must train long hours, averaging between four and five hours per day spread over two workouts, if he expects to reach championship or world-class caliber. He advocates intensive workouts six days per week for high-level competition and suggests that the scholastic wrestler learn all he can about the sport by attending camps and international-style programs, where the fine points of the sport are taught and demonstrated, and wrestle in all styles, including freestyle and Greco-Roman. Stan is emphatic that mental discipline has a significant impact on a wrestler's performance. Like most knowledgeable athletes, Stan urges parents to have patience with their sons and support them fully, especially after they have lost a match.

DAN GABLE

Of the ten premium wrestlers discussed in this chapter, Dan Gable is perhaps the most widely known. After winning the gold medal in the 149.5-pound free-style class at the 1972 Summer Olympics in Munich, he was labeled by many as the best-conditioned athlete and the greatest amateur wrestler in the world.

Dan Gable was appointed University of Iowa's head wrestling coach in 1976, after serving as the Hawkeyes' assistant coach from 1972 to 1976. In 1978 his Big Ten and Midlands Open championship team captured the NCAA champion-ship. In 1979, again under the tutelage of Gable, the Iowa team captured the NCAA championship along with the Big Ten and Midlands Open titles. In 1980, the Iowa Hawkeyes won their third successive national title under the superbly-coached Gable team. In 1980, Dan was elected to the National Wrestling Hall of Fame.

Dan began wrestling when in the fifth grade, although his interest in the sport began at an even earlier age. While wrestling for the Waterloo West High School in Iowa in the 95, 103, and 112-pound classes, he was three times state cham-pion and accumulated a perfect record of 64 wins, 0 losses, and 0 ties.

At Iowa State University, he compiled the unbelievable record of 181–1–0. In March 1970, he was presented the U.S. Amateur Wrestling Foundation's eighth annual award as "Man of the Year" for 1969. This was during his junior year, when his record was 30 and 0 and he had 28 pins (93 percent of his matches). It was during his senior year when he experienced his only collegiate loss—in the

Figure 10-1 Dan Gable shouting instructions to one of his wrestlers during a University of Iowa match.

finals of the NCAA tournament. Since that time, Gable has won titles in the Pan-American Games, the prestigious Russian Tbilisi Tournament, and the World Championships. He was named the U.S.W.F.'s outstanding wrestler in 1971.

The favorite and most-used holds that resulted in his great success included the near-arm far-leg and underhook series. From the control position, he liked the arm-bars. Needless to say, although these were his favorite holds, he efficiently used many different holds in a rhythmic sequence.

Gable, as are the vast majority of real "class" wrestlers, is a proponent of clean living, intensive training, and superb conditioning. He advises young scholastic wrestlers that they can be as good as their natural ability, which can be extended far more than most believe. He advises parents to provide their sons with every opportunity to achieve their top capabilities. (See Figure 10-1.)

LEE KEMP

Lee Kemp began wrestling as a freshman in Chardon, Ohio, at the age of 14, in the 132-pound class. He wrestled on the varsity team all four years, moving up to the 138-pound class his junior year and the 145-pound class his senior year. Throughout his high-school career, he accumulated an 80–10–3 record.

At the University of Wisconsin, he established eight Wisconsin wrestling records, including best career record (143–6–1), best season record (39–0), and most career falls (33). He became the first black wrestler to win three NCAA crowns (1976, 1977, 1978).

Figure 10-2 Lee Kemp in action during a World Championship tournament match.

In the 1978 World Championships in Mexico City, Kemp became the seventh U.S. wrestler to capture a world title. For his outstanding performance in Mexico City, he was named Amateur Wrestling's "Man of the Year" for 1978. Then, in 1979 in San Diego, Kemp again won the 163-pound world title. That same year he was the Pan-American Games gold medalist. In 1979 and 1980, he also claimed individual titles in the World Cup in free-style wrestling. In the winter of 1981, Lee headed the AAU/USA National Team that toured the Soviet Union.

Lee Kemp seems to have no single favorite hold. Rather, he executes a sequence in a smooth rhythmic style that invariably ends up in either a takedown or a predicament. He seems to use single-leg attacks especially effectively. He has also proven to be an artist at defensive wrestling, where he will counter with an arm-drag-to-head outside series or a duck-under followed by a double-leg takedown.

Lee Kemp advises young wrestlers to seek out the best and follow their patterns. He also recognizes the importance of mental discipline and feels that, because of his ability to concentrate, he can command his body to be responsive to the rigors of the sport.

He is quick to suggest that parents continually support their sons, regardless of their performance, by sending them to summer camps and clinics. "Encourage them at all times but do not put pressure on them by stating that they must win" is his advice. (See Figure 10-2.)

MARK T. LIEBERMAN

Mark Lieberman, graduate assistant coach at Lehigh University, continues to be a post-college contender in national and international competition. He began wrestling in eighth grade and continued through high school (Blair Academy in New Jersey), where he was three times a national prep champ in the 158, 168, and 188-pound classes.

In 1977 he finished second in the NCAA championship, which he won in both 1978 and 1979 in the 177-pound class. He placed first in the U.S. Wrestling Federation Nationals in 1978, 1979, and 1980 in the 180.5-pound class. In 1978 in Toledo, Ohio, he won the World Cup championship in the 180.5-pound class.

While wrestling for Lehigh University in the 177 class, he won the Eastern Intercollegiate Wrestling championship four years in succession. In this competition, he was the recipient of the Fletcher Award for the most EIWA career points and the Billy Sheridan Award for the most falls in the least time (four in 9:48). He was also named the Outstanding Wrestler in the 1979 tournament, thus being the first wrestler ever to win all three of these prestigious awards in the history of the EIWA.

Mark's favorite holds are a combination that begins with a duck-under and follows with a power-trip to gain control. He has stated: "I'm not a super-talented individual, I'm not super-quick, super-strong, or super-balanced. But, I plug away. I think that's important." When asked what he feels is the principal reason for his success as a wrestler, he responds quietly: "The God-given blessing of a strong supportive family and three outstanding coaches. Mike Lieberman (my older brother, NCAA champ at 177-pounds in 1975), Thad Turner (the Lehigh University coach, who has been absolutely fantastic for me),

Figure 10-3 Mark Lieberman working for a pin against Jim Kleinhans during the 1979 NCAA championship quarter-finals (photo by Bernhard J. Suess).

and Tommy Hutchinson (the coach of Blair Academy)."

His major advice to young scholastic wrestlers is to learn to love the sport and keen competition. He suggests that young men establish high standards and goals and expect a long and strenuous road in their attainment.

Coming from a family that has been most supportive of his athletic endeavors, he had the following comment to make: "My parents are two of the people I respect most in the world. Without my family, I would have had little success. Parents should never push, they should do as mine—be always supportive and loving and happy with their son's performance." (See Figure 10-3.)

BEN PETERSON

Ben Peterson, wrestling coach and architectural drafting instructor at Maranatha Baptist Bible College, Watertown, Wisconsin, like his brother John, is the recipient of both the silver and gold medals in Olympic competition. In 1972, he was the 198-pound champion in Munich and four years later in Montreal he won the silver medal. Ben earned his spot on the 1980 Olympic team at 198, thus becoming the fourth U.S. wrestler to be a member of three U.S. Olympic teams.

He began wrestling while in high school at the age of 14 in the 180-pound class and finished second in the state of Wisconsin in 1968. While at Iowa State University, he wrestled on two NCAA championship teams and co-captained the 1972 team. He was three-time Big 8 champion and two-time NCAA champion (1971 and 1972) at 190 pounds. Ben was a member of the U.S. World Team in

122

Figure 10-4 Ben Peterson displaying the gold medal he won in the 1972 Olympics.

1973, when he placed third, and in 1975, when he placed fourth. In 1975 he was the Pan-American Games champion.

In competition he primarily used the double-leg takedown and resorted to arm-bars for point accumulation and pinning combinations. When preparing for competition, he includes daily workouts that incorporate weight lifting, running, and hard wrestling. Like his older brother John, Ben feels his Christian boyhood habits have done much to provide him with the mental discipline that results in his success.

His words of advice to aspiring young athletes is to be patient, work faithfully under your coach, and never give up—especially when you experience failure. Ben cautions parents to be very patient with their sons and never let them think they are failures if they don't perform well in early competition. (See Figure 10-4.)

JOHN A. PETERSON

John A. Peterson, wrestling coach with Athletes in Action, did not establish his current image of a supreme wrestler until his college days at Stout State (Wisconsin) had ended. While wrestling for the Cumberland, Wisconsin, high school in the 138 and 154-pound classes, he never made it past the regionals.

Figure 10-5 John Peterson (courtesy Amateur Wrestling News).

And, while wrestling at the 160 and 167-pound classes at the University of Wisconsin at Stout, his best national effort was fifth in the NAIA tournament.

It was not until 1971 that John Peterson decided that he had the physical and mental equipment to succeed in the Olympic Games. Wrestling at the 180.5 class, John captured the silver medal in 1972 at Munich and the gold in 1976 at Montreal. He lost his bid for the 1980 Olympic team at the 180.5-pound class to Chris Campbell, former Iowa two-time NCAA champion. He told the authors that, in preparation for a championship match, he concentrates on the reality of the situation. He knows he is in top physical condition, has the quickness, dexterity, strength, and moves to succeed. He also indicated that his mental discipline is such that he is able to continue to push himself, even though his body tells him he is very tired.

His most productive move has been the double-leg takedown. He accomplishes this move by initiating a single-leg grasp followed by a penetrating step while locking his hands around the opponent's thighs.

John Peterson's major advice to the young scholastic wrestler is to work harder in preparation for the contest than his opponent. He also told the authors that the principal reason for his success is because of his self-control, resulting from a commitment to a Christian life. He wisely cautions parents never to put pressure on their sons to win. He believes that winning in life is more important than winning wrestling matches.

RICK SANDERS

Rick Sanders was the first American to win a World Free-style Wrestling Championship. Tragically, he died at the age of 27 as a result of an automobile accident in Skopje, Yugoslavia, on October 18, 1972. This accident occurred less than two months after he received his second Olympic silver medal.

During his four-year collegiate wrestling career at Portland State University (1965–1968) he compiled an overall record of 103 wins and 2 losses. He won three NCAA College Division and two University Division national titles. At both national tournaments in 1967, he was named the outstanding wrestler. During his freshman year, he won the NAIA championship and at this tournament was also named the outstanding wrestler. He also won four NAAU titles.

In 1969 in Mar del Plata, Argentina, he won the World Championship title in the 114.5-pound class. He had been on the United States World teams of 1964, 1965, 1966, 1967, and 1969, winning the bronze medal in 1967 and the silver in 1968.

In the 1968 Olympic Games in Mexico City, he won the silver medal in the flyweight division, and captured the silver again in the bantamweight division of the 1972 Olympics in Munich. In 1977 he was added to the Amateur Wrestling Hall of Fame.

U.S. Free-style Coach, Bill Farrell, stated: "Rick Sanders was the best wrestler in the world at 125 . . . it won't be easy to forget him and his unusual ways. Certainly, all younger wrestlers in this country looked up to him because of his abilities."

WADE SCHALLES

Of the ten outstanding wrestlers that were selected to be discussed in this book, Wade Schalles, currently head wrestling coach at Clemson.University, has participated in more competition than any other. His overall record of 780 wins, 50 losses, and 1 draw (at the time of this writing) is a record in itself. This performance has been listed in the Guiness Book of World Records.

He has been perhaps the most colorful and unorthodox wrestler that the authors have known. Wade continually seeks and very frequently achieves the fall. In his overall record, he has pinned 60 percent of his opponents (496 pins in 831 matches).

Wade began wrestling at the age of 14 in the 120-pound class. His overall high-school record was 48–2–0, with 42 pins (84 percent of his matches). He won the state championship in Pennsylvania during his senior year (in the 154-pound class), while representing Hollidaysburg High School.

His college record was 153–5–1 with 106 pins (67 percent). His total of 106 pins is the current NCAA record. As a junior at Clarion State, he was voted "Outstanding Wrestler" in the NCAA championships at the University of Maryland in 1972. He won the same honor in the College Division tournament held earlier that same year at Oswego State in the 150-pound competition. Because of his outstanding performance that year, he scored high in the balloting for Amateur Wrestling's "Man of the Year" for 1972. He again captured the NCAA championship in 1973 in the 158-pound division at the University of Washington.

In 1977 he won the National Open free-style championship at 163 pounds and was named the outstanding wrestler of the tournament. That same year in Sofia, Bulgaria, he dominated his class in the World University Games wrestling championships, taking the gold medal in free-style at 163 pounds with five falls and one 16–2 decision. In these games, he was named the outstanding wrestler. Today, he holds the world's record for the most wins and most pins by an amateur wrestler.

Wade Schalles has proved to be a real master of defensive takedowns. After he has the takedown, he immediately goes for the fall with his favorite holds— which primarily include cradles and reverse head-locks.

He attributes his success as a wrestler to developing the ability to anticipate his opponent's moves, thus putting himself in a position to utilize his strategy of defensive takedowns. He prepares for each match by considering all alternatives his opponent will probably utilize and his own counters that will result in his dominance of the situation.

Wade advises young wrestlers to seek the best competition possible by attending Olympic and other training camps that attract the quality athlete. "Do not fear being defeated, but identify each contest as a learning situation," he suggests.

He advises parents to become a qualified student of the game prior to endeavoring to give their sons advice and counsel related to the sport. He also cautions

Figure 10-6 Wade Schalles on his way to winning a gold medal at the 1977 World University Games.

parents to be patient with their sons and support them in connection with their athletic endeavors.

Wade Schalles is a colorful wrestler who continues to compete. (See Figure 10-5.)

ELLIOTT GRAY SIMONS

Elliott Gray Simons, currently head wrestling coach at the University of Tennessee, was a four-time NAIA champion and three-time NCAA champion at Lock Haven State College (Pennsylvania), and was named outstanding wrestler in six of these tournaments, 1959 through 1962. He was a member of the 1960 and 1964 U.S. Olympic free-style teams. In four years of wrestling at Lock Haven, he forged an amazing collegiate record of 91–2. When his collegiate career concluded in 1962, he had 84 consecutive victories. He was elected to the United Savings-Helms Hall Amateur Wrestling Hall of Fame in 1971. In 1978 he was inducted into the National Wrestling Hall of Fame.

It was at the age of 14 that Gray Simons began wrestling in the 95-pound class at Granby High School in Norfolk, Viginia, under the tutelage of Billy Martin. He wrestled throughout his high-school career and accumulated a 41–3 record while wrestling at the 95, 103, 112, and 120-pound weight classes.

Relatively unknown when he arrived at Lock Haven in 1958, Simons did not remain so for long. Under the coaching of Hubert Jack, Gray soon obtained national recognition with his near-perfection moves and fine execution of the "granby roll." He repeatedly accumulated points and falls with the heel pick, duck-under, and the Granby cradle.

Between his sophomore and junior years, Simons became the youngest member of the 1960 Olympic wrestling team and placed fifth in the 114.5-pound class, while beating the world champion from Russia. In the 1964 Olympics, he served as team captain. Under the complex international scoring system, Simons went out of the competition in the fourth round without ever losing a match.

Competing for the New York Athletic Club in the 1964 National AAU Championships, he took first place at 125.5 pounds over five other national champions in that weight class. He went on to serve as an assistant coach at the United States Military Academy and took a gold medal in the World Military Championships in Cairo.

Coaching was a natural step for one of the country's finest wrestlers, and as a head coach Simons has created successful teams for Lock Haven State College, Indiana State University, and the University of Tennessee.

Gray believes that the most important factors for success in wrestling are mental discipline and good coaching. In giving advice to young wrestling hopefuls, he suggests that the best preparation is to consider every match wrestled as being a championship situation. He feels that parents and loved ones should encourage and not criticize their sons. They should recognize that much hard work is essential in preparing to be a champion and that this hard work is softened and made easier if encouragement from loved ones is continually received.

WAYNE WELLS

Wayne Wells, of the University of Oklahoma, reached the pinnacle of competitive wrestling by winning the world championship in the summer of 1970 in Edmonton, Canada. He was the only gold medal winner for the United States in the World Games, and he was voted "Man of the Year" in amateur wrestling for 1970. During that year, he became the first contestant ever to take the "triple crown" of post-graduate wrestling, winning the U.S. Wrestling Federation and U.S. Amateur Wrestling Association (AAU) national championships and capping these with the world crown. In all of these championships, Wayne participated in the 163-pound class.

While a law student at the University of Oklahoma, he had a 69–4–2 collegiate record in the 152-pound class. He was three-time Big Eight champion. In 1968 he captured the NCAA crown and that same year placed fourth in the Olympic Games at Mexico City. The following year (1969), he placed second in the world tournament. In 1972 he won the Olympic gold medal in Munich in the 163-pound class. Wayne Wells is a product of John Marshall High School in Oklahoma City, where he began wrestling at the age of 13. During high school, he wrestled in the 123, 136, and 141-pound classes, and his record was 73 wins, 4 losses, and 1 draw.

Wayne's favorite moves included the Granby roll and the bar nelson. In preparation for a match, he would mentally review his offensive moves and how he would handle certain situations as they developed. Wayne believed in the "power of prayer," and he never began a match until he had "broken a sweat" through adequate warm-up.

In order of importance, he attributes his success to the following: family support, good coaching, strength, and skill. He suggests that young scholastic wrestlers learn the elements of wrestling that best fit their own body and mind and not try to emulate someone else's style. He also emphasizes the importance of strength development and of keeping in good condition the entire year. Wayne advises parents to suggest, not to push. He advocates that they should commend upon winning but never criticize when a loss occurs.

Wells currently practices law in his hometown of Oklahoma City.

SUMMARY

What can be learned from these great wrestlers of the modern era? What advice have they offered regarding preparation, mental discipline, style, etc., to help the young wrestling hopeful? The principal advice that continually crops up is to learn as much about the sport as possible from the coach and to participate in tough competition as often as possible. The next factor to which they attribute success in wrestling is the ability to develop mental toughness or concentration so that the body is commanded by the mind to do its best no matter how fatigued. The third point that appears regularly in their comments is the necessity for complete physical fitness brought about by intensive regular workouts and clean living. These workouts must include much wrestling with superior performers. Finally, all of these champions have advised parents to never put undue pressure on their sons, but to always support them in their athletic endeavors. This support should not decrease when a loss has been suffered, but rather should be intensified. Parents should endeavor to become qualified students of the sport so that they can play a realistic supportive role, giving proper advice and counsel.

It is of special interest that the majority of these wrestlers did not begin the sport until about age 14. This is a good indiciation that it is not necessary to start wrestling at a very early age (for example, in Little League competition) in order to become a champion.

Recommended References

"American College of Sports Medicine Position Stand on Weight Loss in Wrestlers." *Medicine and Science in Sports,* 8, 2 (1976):11–12.

Bubb, Robert G. "Survey of Injuries to Interscholastic Wrestlers in Selected Pennsylvania High Schools, 1966–1967 Season." M.Ed. thesis, The Pennsylvania State University, 1967.

Buskirk, E. R. "Some Nutritional Considerations in the Conditioning of Athletes." *Annual Review of Nutrition,* 1 (1981):319–50.

Buskirk, E. R. "Weight Loss in Wrestlers." *Journal of Diseases in Children,* 132 (April 1978):355–56.

Camaione, David N., and Tillman, Kenneth G. *Teaching and Coaching Wrestling: A Scientific Approach.* 2nd edition. New York: John Wiley & Sons, 1980.

Cooley, Donald G., and Zukerman, Paul. *Family Medical Guide.* New York: Better Homes and Gardens, Inc., 1975.

Gibney, Richard. "Safety In Individual and Dual Sports." *Sports Safety Monographs 4.* Washington, D.C.: American School and Community Safety Association, American Alliance for Health, Physical Education, and Recreation, 1977:12, 43–46.

Gregg, W. H. *Physical Fitness Through Sports and Nutrition.* New York: Scribners, 1975.

Hanson, Norman C. "Wrestling with Making Weight." *The Physician and Sportsmedicine,* 6 (April 1978):107.

Katch, F. I., and McArdle, W. D. *Nutrition, Weight Control, and Exercise.* Boston: Houghton–Mifflin, 1977.

Keen, Clifford P.; Speidel, Charles M.; and Swartz, Raymond H. *Championship Wrestling.* Annapolis, Md.: U. S. Naval Institute, 1967.

Keith, Art. *Complete Book of Wrestling Drills and Conditioning Techniques.* West Nyack, N.Y.: Parker Publishing Co., 1976.

Konrad, Ignatius John. "A Study of Wrestling Injuries in High Schools Throughout Seven Midwest States." Master's thesis, Michigan State University, 1951.

Kraft, Ken. *Mastering Wrestling.* Chicago: Contemporary Books, Inc., 1977.

Lincoln, Ann. *Food for Athletes.* Chicago: Contemporary Books, Inc., 1979.

Lloyd, Frank S.; Deaver, George G.; and Eastwood, Floyd R. *Safety in Athletics.* Philadelphia: W. B. Saunders Co., 1959.

Martens, Rainer; Christina, Robert W.; Harvey, John S. Jr.; Sharkey, Brian. *Coaching Young Athletes.* Champaign, Ill.: Human Kinetics, 1981.

McGinness, Fritz L., ed. *1981–82 National Federation Edition, Wrestling Rules.* Elgin, Ill.: National Federation of State High School Associations, 1981.

NCAA Wrestling Guide, 1982. Shawnee, Kans.: National Collegiate Wrestling Association, annually.

Rasch, Philip J., and Kroll, Walter. *What Research Tells the Coach about Wrestling.* Washington, D.C.: American Association for Health, Physical Education, and Recreation, 1964.

Reek, Claude C. "A National Study of Incidence of Accidents in High School Wrestling." *Research Quarterly,* 10 (March 1939):72–73.

Sasahara, Shozo. *Fundamentals of Scientific Wrestling.* Tokyo: published by the author (4–27 Yoyogi, Shibuya-ku), 1968.

Sciacchetano, Larry, and McCullum, Jack. *Sports Illustrated Wrestling.* Philadelphia: J. B. Lippincott Co., 1979.

Smoll, Frank L., and Smith, Ronald E. "Psychologically-Oriented Coach Training Program: Design, Implementation, and Assessment." *Annual Publication of the North American Society for the Psychology of Sport and Physical Activity.* Champaign, Ill.: Human Kinetics, 1980:112–29.

Tcheng, Tso Kia, and Tipton, Charles M. "Iowa Wrestling Study: Anthropometric Measurements and the Prediction of a 'Minimal' Body Weight for High School Wrestlers." *Medicine and Science in Sports,* 5, 1 (1973):1–10.

Valentine, Tom. *Inside Wrestling.* Chicago: Contemporary Books, Inc., 1972.

Warren, Larry. *1980 AAU Rulebook/Handbook.* Corydon, Ind.: Amateur Athletic Union, 1980.

Wettstone, Eugene, ed. *Gymnastics Safety Manual.* 2nd edition. University Park, Pa.: The Pennsylvania State University Press, 1979.

Wilmore, J. H. *Athletic Training and Physical Fitness.* Boston: Allyn and Bacon, 1976.

The Young Wrestler. Oklahoma City, Okla.: Amateur Wrestling News, Inc. (P.O. Box 1936, zip 73101), monthly.